I0897637

# A Darkness
# at Dawn

*Appalachian Kentucky and the Future*

HARRY M. CAUDILL

THE UNIVERSITY PRESS OF KENTUCKY

Research for The Kentucky Bicentennial Bookshelf
is assisted by a grant from the
National Endowment for the Humanities.
Views expressed in the Bookshelf do not
necessarily represent those of the Endowment.

# Contents

# 1

# THE BEGINNING
# OF IT ALL

Every person and society is a product of two factors, genes and culture. The workings of each is still poorly understood if, indeed, it is understood at all. A culture—the subconsciously and deeply ingrained "truths," mores, prejudices, biases, superstitions, and preferences that link a people together—can bind as surely as shackles of steel. But as those bonds are forged slowly over many generations so they outlast steel, enduring until their origins are lost in the shadowy mists of a common beginning. In Kentucky, folk memories go back to Virginia, North Carolina, and Maryland, but these were only way stations on a protracted journey that carried our ancestors from ancient lands "beyond the waters," and saw some of their descendants continue the trek to the blue Pacific. For those who went on and for those who remained in the Appalachian labyrinth it is important that we ponder our beginnings, for Americans are all descended from immigrants. And each wave of newcomers was, in its time, composed mainly—as Emma Lazarus phrased it so well—of "huddled masses yearning to breathe free."

Anyone who has visited the Tower of London and seen the incredible trappings of pomp and power accumulated by England's Norman kings to cow and overawe the common people may have stared at one of the keys to understanding Appalachian Kentucky. Many deeply rooted attitudes that still give rise to poverty and resignation may have been instilled in the mountaineers' ancestors during the centuries preceding the first English voyage to the New World.

Like nearly all Americans, Kentucky mountaineers are of mixed and varied stock. The names and faces betray bloodlines from French, German, Scottish, and Irish sources, along with goodly inflows of the ubiquitous Ulstermen, the "Scotch-Irish." In fact so distinguished an observer as Arnold Toynbee has erroneously claimed that the Appalachian hills are inhabited almost entirely by the latter.

There are ethnical mysteries to which time apparently has lost the answers. The first of these is the origin of the Melungeons, the fascinating "dark people" who bear English names but claim descent from the "Portagees." Then there are the strong admixtures of Indian blood drawn from the Cherokee and Choctaw tribes, strains almost never encountered in the Bluegrass and farther west. Arched noses, coppery complexions, high cheekbones, and jet-black hair attest to enclaves of aboriginal people who remained to mix their genes with those of white settlers.

But unless I am mistaken, all these strains together—French, German, Irish, Scottish, Ulstermen, Melungeon, and Indian—involve somewhat less than half of the total population. The majority, I believe, came from England, have English names, and have imprinted the region with enduring early-English attitudes.

Generations of old-style politicians regaled crowds of mountain people with assurances that they were the "purest Anglo-Saxon stock" to be found anywhere in the world. There may have been some measure of truth in these trite, oft-repeated claims because more scholarly observers have noted that in cultural matters—ballads and songs, tales and riddles, modes of dancing, and peculiarities of speech—the mountaineer tradition is rooted in Elizabethan England. In these vital respects English influences appear to predominate so overwhelmingly as practically to eradicate other cultural traces.

That Americans are in love with the concept of royalty is attested by millions of framed "family coats of arms" hanging on living room walls. We seek reasons to believe our ancestors were highborn people of substance who, out of religious conviction and in search of freedom, marched together—husband, wife, and children—down to the docks, paid their fare to the skipper, and settled down in their ample but tempest-tossed quarters until the sturdy vessel set them ashore in the Land of Opportunity. According to this fantasy the brave newcomers promptly marched off to wild lands in an ever-receding West, built schools and churches, and continued being and begetting the same kind of solid, dependable citizens they had been in the chivalric Old World. With few exceptions these notions are totally at variance with the facts. Most of us are descended from destitute people who, out of sheer necessity, made a cold and bitter crossing and a fearful and uncertain start on a hard and unfamiliar new continent. In *The Uprooted* Oscar Handlin has described with great discernment the late migrations that filled our cities in the last quarter of the nineteenth century and the first two decades of the twentieth. Those uprooted millions who outbred their land base fled to America in search of jobs and bread. It is less well known that similar convulsions wracked Europe in much earlier times and propelled across the Atlantic ragged multitudes who otherwise would have perished.

Goldsmith's *The Deserted Village* tells the story from the viewpoint of a discerning and sympathetic Englishman. Goldsmith (1728-1774) lived through turbulent years that saw the commons fenced, swarms of people swept off the land by landlords avaricious for sheep pastures, and the cities packed with the dispossessed seeking jobs in the primitive mines, mills, and factories.

3

He saw, too, the populations of whole villages carried away in their tears and sorrow to "a dreary scene, where half the convex world intrudes between."

His description of the American Southland mirrors the Englishman's conception of the hell to which economic pressures were inexorably condemning so many of his countrymen:

> Through torrid tracts with fainting steps they go,
> Where wild Altama murmurs to their woe.
> Far different there from all that charmed before,
> The various terrors of that horrid shore,–
> Those blazing suns that dart a downward ray,
> And fiercely shed intolerable day;
> Those matter woods where birds forget to sing,
> But silent bats in drowsy clusters cling;
> Those poisoned fields with rank luxuriance crowned,
> Where the dark scorpion gathers death around;
> Where at each step the stranger fears to wake
> The rattling terrors of the vengeful snake;
> Where crouching tigers wait their hapless prey,
> And savage men more murderous still than they;
> While oft in whirls the mad tornado flies,
> Far different these from every former scene,
> The cooling brook, the grassy-vested green,
> The breezy covert of the warbling grove.

This is hardly the promised land the folklore of a later time has painted, and they were stricken villagers indeed who came in unnumbered thousands as indentured servants, redemptioners, transported felons and misdemeanants, and evicted tenants shipped off by landlords who nurtured some little spark of compassion.

The dispossessed Englishmen of those days were a far cry from the other streams of humanity that were flowing with them from Europe. The Scottish highlanders expelled by the clearances were products of a long and intimate association with their lairds and tempered by centuries of bloody border warfare. The Germans had been hardened by the turmoil and vicissitudes of the Thirty Years War. The French Huguenots, too, had endured decades of warfare and that crucible had toughened them for the American backwoods. The Scotch-Irish, impoverished by parliamentary enactments against their religion and wool trade, brought an implacable hatred of England and a self-reliance honed by generations on the perilous frontier of the "Ulster plantation." All these people had certain qualities in common: they were dissenters against the established order, had struggled to maintain their principles and possessions, and were prepared to enter their new environment with audacity and confidence. The upheavals and turmoil through which they passed had sharpened their determination without dulling their deeply ingrained work ethic. They had more than a passing knowledge of the stratagems and techniques of warfare and their essential psychology enabled them to adapt quickly to brawling frontier conditions. It is not surprising, then, that as the line of settlements crept toward the Appalachians and then spilled over into the Kentucky Bluegrass and beyond, the names of the great scouts and organizers and their irrepressible followers were overwhelmingly non-English: Sevier, Croghan, Harman, Shelby, Campbell, Kenton, Boone, Harrod, McKee, Clark, Robertson, Salling, Holston, Mansker, Bledsoe, Girty, Gist, LaMothe, Chartier, McGary, Cresap, Ecuyer, Hogg, Finley, Sowdowski, Skaggs, Calloway, Walden, Stoner, Coulter.

What, then, became of all the English people who poured across the Atlantic in the century before the Revolution? Dale Van Every has described the frontiersmen as "a heterogeneous population of Germans, Scotch-Irish, somewhat fewer English, and a sprinkling of Welsh and Huguenot French." They were, he writes, "wretchedly poor" and most had come as redemptioners or indentured servants. It is reasonable to surmise that the poor English whom John Fiske has referred to as "mean English" were, in the main, simply unprepared to dash off to the frontier, live in a dirt-floored cabin or brush shack, subsist on parched corn and the flesh of wild beasts, and endure the constant peril of Indian attack and death by torture. Feudalism had made them chattels bound to the land and in later times class distinctions and prejudices tied the destitute commoner to his social place, a forelock-tugging, obsequious, landless neo-serf. He subsisted by the generosity of landlord or employer and was respectful of his "betters," a characteristic that crops out to this day when reverential subjects gasp in adoration at a glimpse of the queen. Their low social status, economic dependence, and long-ingrained caste-consciousness had turned the impoverished English masses into psychological invalids, adept as plowmen and day laborers but filled with understandable caution when called upon to rout Indians out of a vast and gloomy wilderness.

If John Fiske was right, we may surmise that the flood of "mean English" who came to Virginia were unable or unwilling to compete effectively in the thriving society of the Old Dominion. There are many exceptions, as there are to most rules, but mainly they shrank from the turbulent frontier where people were bleeding in interminable wars, yet found it practically impossible to sell their labor for a living wage in competition with black slaves. The vast grants of Virginia land to royal favorites made it difficult for these depressed classes to acquire farms for themselves in a settled district. Consequently redemptioners whose terms were out, others who fled to avoid further service, and freemen seeking to become small-holding farmers joined outlaws in flight from the noose and took up their abode in the North Carolina hinterland. There they were safely behind the ravages of the frontier itself and beyond the restrictions and burdens of life in the coastal towns. In this setting they learned to adapt their farming to new conditions of soil and climate, developed a taste for Indian corn, pumpkins, and wild game, and changed, after two or three generations, into Americans as tough and resilient as their compatriots anywhere.

During this period of incubation the Scotch-Irish, Germans, Huguenot French, and the boldest and most adaptive of the English were shoving the frontier westward in pell-mell fashion so that in 1794 with the battle of Fallen Timbers, Indian power was cleared from Kentucky and broken forever in the immense Northwest. This development left the central Appalachians free of the Shawnee, Choctaw, and Cherokee raiders who had struck such terror to the English immigrants and their progeny. The lure of free and safe land set in motion an enormous movement of people into the hilly labyrinth, people who in the main bore such forthright English names as Wright, Mason, Smith, Baker, Banks, Brown, Long, Ward, Thomas, Bentley, Free, Boatwright, Hall, Adams, Wells, Brewer, Fuller, White, Freeman, Rose, Turner, Fletcher, Stamper, Noble, May, Friend, Still, Franklin, Archer, Coldiron, Dyer, Fields, Sexton, Potter, Cook, Johnson, Tanner, Hightower, Hale, Combs, Bishop, Shepherd, Short, Bowman, Dishman, Boggs, Lowman, King, Bowling, Begley, Hatfield, Sizemore, and Collier. The German, Scotch-Irish, and French names were among them too, of course, when this backwater was settled, and were promptly assimilated into the culture fashioned by the majority. The newcomers brought the raw, rough backwoods attitudes to a wild, tumbled land earlier waves of settlers had disdained as "the wilderness." Like a great sponge the Appalachian labyrinth soaked up the settlers, insulating them against the outside world and perpetuating the customs, ideas, mores, attitudes, prejudices, vices, virtues, and traditions they had brought with them.

Most of the family names that sound in the Kentucky hills today were already in America, mainly in Virginia, a full century before Thomas Jefferson took up his quill pen to write the Declaration of Independence. I am, of course, aware that many careful students, including the eminently respectable genealogist William C. Kozee hold to the view that Scotch-Irish is the predominant strain in Appalachia. There is a possibility that they are right, but other evidence is against them. The virtual disappearance of the Ulsterman's religion suggests that his was a lesser influence than is commonly supposed.

The journal of the Reverend James Gilruth of Greenup County published in an Ironton, Ohio, newspaper in 1879 shows how little influence was exerted by religion in the lives of early mountain settlers. He declared that "up to 1818 I haven't the most distant knowledge of there having lived in the place so much as one man, woman or child that made any profession of or gave any evidence of being religiously inclined."

Greenup County was not singular in this respect as indicated by the Big Sandy Valley historian William Ely who notes, for example, that the first wedding in all the valley to take place in a church house was solemnized at Catlettsburg on July 16, 1862—more than eighty years after settlers began moving into the region. This unconcern for organized religion appears to have been a cultural trait that was deeply implanted when the frontier was still two hundred miles to the east or, perhaps, in England where church meant taxes and burdens.

By contrast the lowland Scots whom Elizabeth moved into Ireland's northern counties were almost all devoted Presbyterians. In Ulster they clung to their faith with a passion and when parliament restricted its practice they "crossed the waters" in such numbers that by the beginning of the revolution they amounted to a sixth of the total population. These sons of the Covenanters carried their doctrines and practices with them wherever they moved. Their congregations still dot the North Carolina and Virginia landscape and their progress westward is marked by churches they founded and their descendants have preserved. In both Ulster and Scotland the adherence to Calvinism has continued undimmed through persecutions, deportations, civil wars, clearances, famines, and pestilence. The influence of the church re-

8

mained strong in such new western states as Missouri where people with Scotch-Irish names penetrated in large numbers. But when the tireless Presbyterian evangelist E. O. Guerrant traveled the Kentucky hills during and after the Civil War he found some 90 percent of the inhabitants totally unchurched. Perhaps a tenth belonged to more or less established Baptist congregations, and practically the entire population thought of themselves as adhering to Baptist principles. Presbyterianism was almost wholly unknown even as to the name, and none of its churches were to be found. Allowing for the vast influence of the Baptist revivalist movement in Kentucky at the beginning of the nineteenth century, it is inconceivable that it could have swept away strong Presbyterian churches of the character history associates with the Ulster people. This marked absence of the principal feature of Scotch-Irish life and culture indicates that they were a small minority who yielded to and assimilated with a predominantly Baptist-leaning or irreligious majority. For a strong Scottish element to abandon their church in such a fashion would be without precedent then and now.

Another circumstance that argues against the notion of Scotch-Irish predominance among the settlers of Appalachian Kentucky was their persistent illiteracy. The Ulstermen were, in the main, well schooled by the standards of their time, with a deeply rooted insistence on an educated clergy. For example, Fiske relates that in a document signed in 1718 by a miscellaneous group of 319 men, only 13 made their marks while 306 wrote their names in full. This reflects a level of literacy vastly higher than can be found in most of America to this day. The Scotch-Irish opened schools wherever they went, including Harrodsburg and Boonesboro. ("Wild-Cat" McKenny, Louisville's first teacher, brought learning to that tiny community when "varmints" were, as he was so sharply reminded, a very real menace.) But in the Kentucky mountains the drive for education was extremely

9

weak. Few counties had a school of any kind a half-century after settlers began to arrive. A scattering of log schoolhouses were built in the 1840s but Guerrant saw none two decades later. Notwithstanding the rough terrain and the distances between families, it is hard to suppose that a populace strongly influenced by Scotch-Irish would have lapsed into the unrelieved illiteracy and general ignorance that gripped the region when the "mission teachers" began to arrive eighty years ago.

Such circumstances reflect an original populace that was essentially rootless, deprived by their history of church, schooling, and other established cultural facets. It was a populace that wanted mostly to be left alone and was significantly lacking in the ambition for worldly gain that drove the Scotch-Irish, Huguenots, and Germans, and later the Jews, from Europe's ghettos.

# 2

# HOW SEEDS OF
# TROUBLE BORE FRUIT

THE BACKWOODS culture that was thus set down within the enshielding hills had certain strengths that have endured tenaciously to the present despite the assaults of television, the automobile, and a whole series of socially revolutionary traumas. The first was a sense of place, a strong attachment to familiar valleys with their meandering creeks and cliff-capped hills. The land makes such an attachment easy because the terrain is varied and, to one who looks closely, displays countless distinguishing features. It is a friendly environment with adequate rain, gentle winters, and cool summers. The hills shoulder storms away, and until the generations brought too many mouths the bottomlands and lower slopes yielded ample food. Hence the craving so evident in "briar" and "hillbilly" migrants long transplanted to northern cities to return to the hills on vacations and for retirement.

Another trait is clannishness. The settlers generally came in groups of three or four families who had been friends in the old settlements. They found the broader bottoms, cleared out the wild cane, girdled the trees, and built cabins. They lived close together for such mutually beneficial "workings" as house raisings, log rollings, and, for the wives, the consolation of female companionship in the ordeal of childbearing. As their children matured they found spouses among these neighbors and cemented the bonds of friendship with ties of blood and name. Succeeding generations, too, tended to "marry close to home" in the same manner so that fantastically complex and overlayered consanguinous relationships ensued. Marriages between first cousins were commonplace, and double first cousins were, and are, frequently encountered. Among such groupings assimilation became almost total so that at the end of three or four generations the people tended to look alike, talk with similar inflections, and share the same preferences in food, fiddle tunes, and politics. Thus when a mountaineer returns to his familiar place on the Appalachian earth he moves into a comfortable, intimate social relationship with roots that are now many generations old.

But the faults of the culture outweighed its strengths. In their isolation the clans had none from whom to learn except themselves. Each contributed his own narrow store of experience and wisdom, and since our indentured ancestors came as illiterates they could learn nothing from the printed page. News came only rarely from some itinerant preacher or returning stock-drover. Consequently people looked to themselves, and backwards to folkways, for solutions and remedies. They became exceedingly traditionalistic, endlessly repeating in their housing, farming, and religion the ideas and usages of their forebears. Inevitably they turned to the old for guidance so that society became rigidly patriarchal. The old men, in their narrowness of mind and limitations of experience, became oracles to whom their communities turned for guidance and inspiration. The old men cautioned against the new and untried and counseled a firm adherence to the established and familiar. In this cranky conservatism is rooted a vast part of the troubles that have dogged the highlander from the beginning of his sojourn in the Appalachians.

Another seed of the mountaineer's downfall lay in his

cavalier disregard of "schoolin'." If he ever heard of it he ignored James Madison's great admonition: "Knowledge will forever govern ignorance. And a people who mean to be their own governors must arm themselves with the power knowledge gives. A popular government without popular information or the means of acquiring it is but a prologue to a farce or a tragedy, or perhaps both."

The truth of the great Virginian's warning has been grimly confirmed as mountain people have been battered and baffled by one challenge after another. The settlements were more than half a century old before the first steps toward public schools were forced upon them by faraway state officials. The first collections of ragged scholars assembled inside huge hollow trees or floorless cabins with smoke-holes in lieu of chimneys. They were taught, if that word can be made to apply, by men who themselves could claim few gains in the struggle for literacy. Progress in education advanced with glacial slowness, resisted adamantly by taxpayers whom ignorance had impoverished and who could see no benefit to be derived from so radical a departure from old norms. "My people afore me," it was often observed, "got by without book learnin' and my youngun's don't need none neither!" Thus as their first century within the hills drew to a close and capitalists from New York, London, and Philadelphia came to speculate in Appalachian land, the highland people knew virtually nothing about its intrinsic value or why millions of people in distant cities were destined to become dependent upon its resources. As they had never learned to farm it effectively, they now failed to comprehend the value of its mineral deposits and, in effect, practically donated those riches to the rest of the world. They sold for fifty cents to a dollar per acre what has proved to be among the planet's most valuable natural resource reserves. It seems never to have occurred to anyone in eastern Kentucky to doubt the representations of the speculators and send some trusted young men to the places where such information could be obtained to ferret out the truth about the coal veins, brine beds, oil and gas deposits, and ledges of limestone, iron ore, and silica-rich sands.

Here the name of one Kentucky mountaineer stands out like an Everest towering over a broad expanse of low hills. John Caldwell Calhoun Mayo of Paintsville was a rare combination of keen intelligence, broad vision, boundless ambition, and incredible physical stamina. First as a backwoods schoolteacher and then as a country lawyer he perceived the immensity of his region's natural wealth and its inevitable importance to the future. Without funds of his own and against incredible odds he put together an astonishing industrial and financial empire. He brought the ubiquitous and iniquitous "broad form" mineral deed* to eastern Kentucky and by tirelessly riding thousands of miles in eight counties secured title to tens of thousands of acres. To do so he slept on shuck beds and ate grease-drenched food in numberless cabins on forays that sometimes lasted for many weeks at a stretch. His energy and foresight produced Kentucky River Coal Corporation and Elkhorn Coal Corporation, and his machinations established Northern Coal and Coke and Consolidation Coal in the valleys of the Big Sandy and Kentucky River. His enterprise started railroads into the hills a decade earlier than they might otherwise have come, and his cunning marshaled the power of coal to push through the legislature a series of laws that made possible the east Kentucky coal industry's systematic rape of the entire territory. Hardly able at the beginning of his career to advance even minimal cash considerations for his title options, he built a vast fortune before his death at fifty-one in 1914. His name appears in Kentucky deed books more often than any other, and his home is to this day the only house in all the hills worthy to

*This document was used to "sever" title to the minerals within the land from the "surface estate" and eventually extended to 75 percent of the land in the eastern Kentucky coalfields.

be called a mansion. The Mayo Complex of mansion, church, bank, and office are worth a visit, and as one stands before the pillars of his house or at the huge slab of marble that marks his grave, one is overwhelmed by the magnitude of his achievements. One senses his presence, his compelling personality, still there in the valleys with their endless coal trains, rows of camp houses, and clouds of coal dust and smoke. No other man has had so profound an impact on the economic life of Kentucky, and the forces he organized and set to work still dominate its affairs. Here, for good or ill, was a titan among pigmies, a towering folk hero risen from the people as a volcanic peak sometimes thrusts above the sea.

A childish trust in others has long been a characteristic of the Appalachian mind. It has been noted by many observers that the mountaineer is suspicious of strangers and that, in earlier decades at least, a "furriner" or "outlander" ran certain grave risks simply by venturing into some remote hollow. Such valleys sheltered women who seldom if ever had set foot inside a town, and men and women alike thought of the alien as dangerous. Their conservatism assured such an attitude. At the same time, they lived in a harsh, often brutal backwoods society that afforded few amenities and were grateful when someone showed them attention and kindness. And in every age the strangers who have come to the hills in search of their treasures have been considerate and urbane souls, quick to commend and praise, lavish in their attentions, never so impatient as to lose a deal by overreaching.

The buyers of mineral deeds flattered the mountaineer with expressions of concern for him and his family, made reference to the hill man's shrewdness, saw erudition in his most commonplace achievements. They came to the remote farms under "tongue of good report," then returned again and again until the title deeds bore the scrawled X's that conveyed "all mineral and metallic substances" and, coincidentally, virtual sovereignty over the region as well. Those title deeds beckoned to capital and industry, the smooth-talking agents departed as rich men, and where mountaineers had once ridden their horses came railroads and highways. Bewildered mountaineers saw towns spring up and heard the earth shake in the throes of tremendous enterprises. Having handed over the rights that made it all possible they had no choice but to forsake cornfields and the bright sun of day to dig the glittering lumps they once had owned.

Incredibly, the decades since R. M. Broas, E. B. Moon, John C. C. Mayo, W. J. Horsley, and all the other land agents rode out of the hills have taught most mountaineers little or nothing in dealing with those who come to despoil the land. Their great poplar and walnut trees went the way of their coal veins, and their unblemished white oaks followed to make whiskey barrels for the huge distilleries in Louisville. Today when strip miners and oil drillers bargain for entry rights onto fields and lawns, the invariable result ensues. The man who speaks for the corporation is "mighty nice" or is "a fair talkin' man," and the terms that are worked out are preposterously one-sided. The company gets what it needs and in due time the rueful highlander discovers that his agreement is full of loopholes or, more likely, that the operator had no intention of complying with it in the first place.

In our own blasé and cynical age the mountaineers' willingness to trust others, to "take a man's word as his bond," and, in situation after situation, to suffer disastrous consequences appears unbelievably naive. Even more, it is silly. It has enabled fly-by-night strip miners, for example, to cozen whole communities into accepting mountaintop mining operations which promptly render the watersheds unstable, flood-prone, and subject to gigantic landslides. A promise to "reclaim" the land is generally enough, a promise that a visit to the operator's activities along other creeks would promptly expose as an utter sham. Amazingly, such visits are almost never made with the result that scores of hollows have had to be abandoned by aged inhabitants who now cluster elsewhere in shabby collections of house trailers. This streak of persistent innocence is a cultural characteristic bequeathed by the ancient clan relationship in which people were interdependent and learned at an early age that to deceive was to become an outcast. Thus men trusted because others were trustworthy, a concept that was applied with calamitous consequences when the twentieth century caught up with the eighteenth.

Of all the qualities and attitudes that have contributed to the Appalachian dilemma, the most deadly has been a continuing ignorance of the nature of the land itself. Because he failed to understand his environment the highlander misused and abused it with disastrous consequences to himself and his descendants.

If my conjectures about the origins of our Appalachian forebears are correct, the poor English were reluctant immigrants. They came because they had to, pushed out by poverty and harsh penal laws that punished destitution almost as much as criminality. They came from quiet villages, farms gentled by centuries of cultivation, and in huge numbers from city streets. In the scheme of things as they had always known them, their overlords had told them what to do and had imparted to them such knowledge as they needed to accomplish their tasks. In the harsh, wild environment of America they were cast adrift on their own and simply never got either their bearings or mastery of their situation. They learned certain rudimentary things that enabled them to make a tenuous peace with the land, but they did not learn enough to make that peace endure or to build abiding institutions founded on the soil. They learned mainly from books, and because there was no social hierarchy to teach and direct them within a larger and more disciplined range, they repeated those simple skills acquired from the aborigines long after changing circumstances and increased numbers had rendered them hopelessly obsolete.

They came in contact with the Indians after the lust for trade goods had turned the tribes into commercial peoples who hunted relentlessly. They had to have furs and pelts to exchange for the white man's knives, rifles, gun powder, mirrors, beads, and cotton cloth. In the formative years of their culture our Appalachian forebears, too, learned that beaver and deer skins could be turned to cash and they took up the hunter's calling with all the red man's zeal. Their passion for pursuit of wild creatures did not flag until the deer, black bear, turkeys, and squirrels that once teemed across the coves and along the dark streams had been all but exterminated. Today one can walk for miles through new growths of returning forest and catch scarcely a glimpse of any winged or furry thing, a barren legacy of the time when a bale of pelts could bring a few comforts to a floorless cabin. Many thousands of officers and soldiers in Bonaparte's grande armée wore great coats made from the skins of black bears hunted in the Kentucky hills and shipped by flatboats to New Orleans and thence to France. The first "cash money boom" the hills experienced was fueled by the Colonel DeRossett's frantic buying of these skins at his Louisa trading post.

What was ultimately more ruinous, our ancestors learned their farming from the same humble mentors. European grains did not thrive in stump-dotted, root-choked new grounds, but the squaws taught them to cultivate Indian corn, squashes, beans, and potatoes. Unfortunately they did not know, or soon forgot, how to protect the black virginal leaf-mold soil with cover crops, and it washed away beneath the relentless rains. New fields had to be cleared, and as families grew and multiplied still more lands were required. The white man's plow supplemented the hoe of the squaw, but otherwise few innovations were ever adopted. Trees were deadened or felled, the crops were planted, hoed, and harvested in fields that spread up the creeks and then, in broad splotches, up the slopes into the rich, shade-darkened coves. This agriculture shackled mountaineers in the grip of poverty because erosion swept away the soil they knew no means of protecting or restoring. Within a century the mountain people were in a servitude that bound them to the grubbing hoe and deadening axe, a bondage in which even the most unstinting labor could produce barely enough corn for the meal barrel, for fattening hogs, and for the plow mule. Throughout the nineteenth century Appalachian destitution sent waves of people to settle the South and West and reenact these elements of their culture wherever towns grew up and men cleared lands for plantations, ranches, and farms. In Faulkner's pages we read about some of them and their descendants.

But of all the traits brought from his humble English origins the most devastating was the highlander's deeply rooted mistrust of government. In the Old World, government was regarded as monolithic, overwhelming, and oppressive. It was enthroned in vast palaces, decked in silks and glittering gems, carried in great coaches, and ringed with swords and bayonets. Government taxed men, seized their bodies for service in the army and navy, sent them to jails and workhouses for some crimes and hanged them for others. Government was on the side of the rich, supporting landlords when they evicted ancient communities of farmers and "tumbled" their houses, or seized the commons in defiance of law and custom. Then, when there were more people than the land and its institutions could support, the government found efficient ways of packing off the surplus to the colonies. In the colonies the poor found the same apparatus in firm control, taxing, regulating, punishing. Privilege reigned supreme and unassailable, and to escape its strictures and burdens the poor could find but one hope: they gravitated westward beyond the frontier and eventually into the hills. In their souls they bore a suspicion of government that two centuries of democratic "self-rule" have done little to efface. One of the paradoxes of modern American society lies in the fact that decades after the hill people became dependent on government largesse, subsisting largely on handouts of food and welfare and social security checks, their innate conservatism still sees that same government which sustains them as dangerous and, except on "relief days," to be avoided. This attitude dooms them because progress, even survival, in the modern world requires soundly conceived governmental policies forthrightly and effectively executed. People who use government prosper while people who shrink from it sink. This simple truth explains why the very rich spend so much to support their lobbyists.

Folk memories are exceedingly tenacious, but even in modern times government has done much to deepen the mountaineer's monumental cynicism toward it. A prime example is the workings of the whiskey taxes, going back to George Washington and the "whiskey rebellion." The settlers brought not only a taste for distilled corn but skills in preparing it. After the revolt was broken in Pennsylvania hundreds of distillers moved west, many of them stopping in the hills. The highlander sent whiskey down the river on rafts and flatboats with hogsheads of tobacco, bales of leather, sacks of ginseng, boxes of maple sugar, and jars of wild honey. For decades these commodities and droves of lean cattle and "floats" of logs were his only means of obtaining money or essential goods. But of them all the fiery output of his stills was the most important. He could turn a bushel of corn and some hops into a gallon of whiskey, increasing the value five or six times in the process. At Frankfort or Louisville huge distilling corporations would gauge it, then haggle until it was bought. Stored in charred white-oak barrels until properly aged it would eventually retail as mild and mellow bottled-in bond. This was all very legitimate and profitable, but the system raised difficulties for the federal treasury. Despite tightening laws much of the alcohol trickling from the hundreds of tiny, widely scattered stills brought in no taxes. So Congress effectually outlawed them, abolishing with a roll call the economic underpinnings of thousands of already hard-pressed households.

The stills were what we would today call "cottage industry," as indigenous and uniformly accepted as the loom. The mountaineer resented this assault upon his livelihood as a physician might resent a ban against the practice of medicine, and, to his everlasting credit, he resisted. He fought with cunning, and sometimes with Winchester rifles. Hundreds of men died and thousands went to penitentiaries before law and order prevailed and a dispirited people realized that they had been thoroughly defeated. Mountaineers never forgave the government for outlawing what they knew best how to make, while licensing others to continue making the same substance on a vastly greater scale.

Mountaineers learned their next lesson about the unpredictability of the government after the destruction of their stills and the exhaustion of their croplands drove them into the mines. By its very nature coal mining is exceedingly hazardous, and the United States expended little money or effort to lessen the danger of death or injury that stalked the dark, dusty tunnels.

More often than not the ledge of stone that lies above a coal vein is crumbly and decayed. The strata do not adhere tightly to one another and when the coal is removed roof-falls are triggered, some of them on so large a scale that not even a forest of hickory and black oak props will hold the layers in place. Methane seeps out of the coal and highly volatile dust settles everywhere, awaiting a spark to ignite explosions comparable to dynamite. All these perils dogged the Appalachian miner. Graveyards were filled with crushed and blackened bodies, and cripples hobbled on canes and crutches along the streets of camps and county seats. Widows and orphans accumulated wherever coal was mined. Any discerning person could have testified that this disgraceful carnage was undermining both the Appalachian economy and its society, but nearly a half-century passed before Congress or a president stirred a finger to save the men who provide so much of the nation's heat and energy. Even after World

War II coal-mining states spent more money for game wardens to protect rabbits and squirrels than on inspectors to protect miners.

During World War II the mountaineer's labor fueled the "Great Arsenal of Democracy" that crushed the Axis, and he often worked a month at a stretch without missing a shift, including Saturdays, Sundays, and holidays. He worked with worn tools and under inadequate engineering supervision. His industry enjoyed no wartime subsidies or postwar guarantees—virtually the only major industry to carry this ominous distinction—and after victory he saw the cruel purchasing practices of the Tennessee Valley Authority combine with general governmental indifference and the gross corruption of his labor union to wipe out thousands of jobs in the pits.

In all these vicissitudes miners died by needless thousands in accidents no other industrialized western nation would have tolerated. It is fair to say that in the 1960s the death rate in United States mines would, in the mines of any country in western Europe, have brought down the government. A comparison of the statistics will give any conscientious American cause for shame.

In Belgium, in the ten years after World War II, the death rate per million manshifts underground ranged from a high of 0.66 in 1953 to 0.32 in 1955. In Britain, in those same years the high figure was 0.47 in 1947 and ranged down to 0.24 in 1954. In France the rate was 0.48 in 1948 and 0.34 in 1955. In West Germany, ravaged by years of aerial bombardment, the mortality level declined from 0.77 in 1948 to 0.61 in 1955. In the United States the kill rate was a horrendous 1.22 in 1947 and 0.84 in 1952. In Kentucky as late as 1971 the death rate was 1.13 in large operations and 3.47 in small ones employing fifteen men or fewer. Slave miners in Hitlerite Germany worked under better safety conditions than prevailed in a large sector of the Kentucky coal industry twenty-six years after the collapse of the Nazi empire.

Such lessons were not wholly lost on the mountaineer.

22

These grim experiences imprinted upon him a somber realization that to the people who run the country his life and well-being were of small concern, deepening his cynicism and convincing him anew that government serves mainly the rich and the powerful. Regarding himself as a victim of government, he saw that same government as fair game to be victimized whenever and wherever possible. This attitude, seldom expressed but deeply felt, combined with a bewildering realization of helplessness to turn the mountaineer into an astonishingly adept welfare client. As his economic circumstances declined he turned to the multiplying forms of public assistance and worked them as effectively as once he had used the timber stands and coal veins.

No people in the nation are more forlorn than the Appalachian highlanders in our time. Their bewilderment grows out of a tenacious, deeply rooted, and conservative culture which was abruptly overwhelmed by vast forces that shattered the old without creating a viable system of new values, mores, and relationships.

Long before World War II the land as it was organized and used had been outstripped by numbers. The old practices sent little houses up every major creek, then up the forks of the creek, then up the little branches. Fecundity did not abate, even after the coves were cleared and the black loam of untold millennia had found its watery way to the Mississippi delta. In the agricultural economy the stork outran the grubbing hoe and plow.

The Great Depression that ruined so much of America was, paradoxically, something of a blessing to the highlands. In ever-worsening poverty for nearly a century, the Appalachians had been ignored when they suffered alone, but when the entire nation groaned and the relief trains began to roll, the region shared the general benefits. Because of the work projects of Civil Works Administration, Works Progress Administration, and Public Works Administration, the enrollment of youth in the Civilian Conservation Corps, the stipends issued to students by National Youth Administration, and the endless boxcar loads of free food and clothing, the mountain people were better off in the bleak 1930s. For those dependent on the land the shift to relief, though at first humiliating, brought no increase in hardships. Indeed the provender issuing from "the giveaway" and the small wages paid out by the projects enhanced the security of multitudes who had farmed until, exhausted and baffled, they were at the end of their tether.

Nearly a decade of New Deal style assistance was to pass before bombs crashing into the United States navy at Pearl Harbor roused the economy and restored the mountain people to a modicum of prosperity. By the thousands men, women, and youths packed their meager clothing into cheap suitcases or cardboard boxes and headed outward to jobs in the war industries: to the tank factories of Detroit, the shipyards of Baltimore, the powder plants of Charlestown, Indiana, and Radford, Virginia. The wartime exodus moved more than a million "hillbillies" into the overcrowded and decaying central city slums which had not yet been inundated by multitudes of blacks fleeing the cotton fields. This massive upheaval has left an abiding mark on the American city, exemplified by the wail of country music pounding from countless radio transmitters.

Vast though the exodus was, not all left for the cities and factories. Most stayed behind to dig coal in the immense wartime expansion of the industry, but the boom was only temporary. For decades the oil companies in the South had simply burned or "flared off" the huge flows of gas that poured out of their wells. To bring this fuel to the chill Northeast the federal government subsidized the building of the "little inch" and "big inch" pipelines, and tremendous quantities of this clean fuel began arriving at the homes and offices of people weary of coal soot, dust, and ashes. When the war ended, the rush to gas and oil accelerated as King Coal's throne crumbled.

In the first decade of the twentieth century railroads

were big business—indeed the biggest business in the nation—and trains drawn by steel behemoths consumed prodigious quantities of coal and left soot and foul smells in their wake. They were improved and enlarged versions of the first locomotives, but wartime technology abruptly ended their long reign. New and better diesel plants were essential to the war effort, and federal funds financed sweeping improvements. The size of the engines shrank while their power increased, and by the late 1940s manufacturers were ready with sleek new oil burners. With the collapse of the engine fuel market the eastern Kentucky coal industry practically disintegrated. The catastrophe brought economic calamity exceeding that of the Great Depression, but with a chilling difference: in the 1950s there was no Franklin D. Roosevelt in the White House.

A measure of coal's decline and of the depression that tumbled into the coal country can be gained from the abrupt fall of production. In 1947 United States pits produced 631 million tons. In 1949 the total was 438 million tons. Kentucky's drop was even more precipitous.

# 3

# THE TYRANNY OF COAL

Grown complacent and prosperous in seven fat years, mining companies were stunned as nearly half their markets vanished within a three-year span. Loaded gondolas piled up at the tipples, then were sold for less than cost. Price-cutting garnered orders that merely deepened the distress. Expenses had to be reduced and always precarious safety precautions were curtailed. The industry declared war on the United Mine Workers of America and, in a decade of new strife, managed to drive the half-starved men out of the union and into the pits at less than half their former wages. Many operations allowed Workmen's Compensation insurance contracts to lapse. But despite the retrenchments, mining corporations fell like weeds before a sickle. The investments of stockholders and the livelihood of workmen evaporated together. In hollow after hollow trains ceased to run, tipples rotted and rusted, boarded-up company stores sagged into ruin, and entire rows of houses were abandoned to bats and vandals. Never in American history was an industry so battered as was Appalachian coal in the decade of the 1950s.

At this juncture the Tennessee Valley Authority (TVA) administered the coup de grace. This gigantic agency had been created by Congress to conserve and rebuild the eroded valley of the Tennessee River, to harness the turbulent stream with dams, and to generate hydroelectricity for the enhancement of the region's economy. The scheme worked so well that in less than twenty years its customers had outrun the capacity of its water-turned turbines, and TVA turned to coal-powered plants. A string of colossal thermal installations was built and the agency became the nation's largest coal consumer, burning about 5 percent of the country's total output.

In the beginning TVA was conservation oriented. Its nitrogen-fixation plants provided trainloads of free fertilizer for the gullied hills and its nurseries produced free seedlings for tree plantations. The fields turned from a ghastly yellow to a glistening green. Then in the 1950s TVA abruptly changed direction. Its original primary concern with people and resources was dropped and it became simply an immense government-owned electric power corporation. The new managers adopted all the vices of the private power industry, sometimes displaying even less interest in the land affected by their far-flung operations than their compatriots in the investor-owned companies.

With these titanic coal-fired furnaces TVA became exceedingly cost-conscious, striving to supply at the lowest possible cost all the power needed by its lengthening list of prospering customers. Deep mines could not meet the agency's price requirements. After wages fell to six or eight dollars a day and the companies were willing to settle for little more than operating expenses, the pitiless accountants demanded still cheaper fuel.

TVA adopted the practice of advertising for bids on a specified quantity of coal, then awarding only a portion of the order to the lowest bidder. Its spokesmen would point out that the bid exceeded expectations and would mention a more suitable price. When new bids were opened the desperate operators would have pared their prices still further. Haggard miners dragged the coal out of the hills amid increasing carnage and social and economic disintegration. The companies slid ever deeper into financial ruin and scores of names linked to the coalfield since the laying of the railroads sold out and moved away rather than continue to struggle against what they believed to be insurmountable difficulties.

But not all surrendered so easily. As the old order based on deep mines and hand labor dissolved, new men came to build fortunes out of the same coal veins, but using new tools and techniques. They were strip miners who used immense diesel-powered shovels, augers, and bulldozers to take a mountain apart for its coal in an inexpensive operation requiring few employees. Since TVA was willing to sign long-term contracts, the machinery makers could afford to sell their costly tools on credit. New corporations sprang up with millions of dollars worth of contracts and a burning determination to get rich. TVA thus cold-bloodedly decreed the destruction of a broad region adjacent to the territory it was mandated to protect in order to supply its customers with the cheapest electricity in the world.

TVA got the cheap fuel it demanded, and other utilities and steel companies copied these tactics to obtain the same benefits for themselves. Deep-mining operations disappeared like a sandy creek bank sawed by a flash flood. Starvation and rags reached epidemic proportions, the federal food dole was restored, and outmigration carried the brightest and best out of the hills. Streams filled with mud from the flayed and decapitated ridges, while gargantuan mud slides routed countless families from their homes. State and federal agencies sent teams to study the horrendous blight that had descended on Appalachia. TVA balance sheets glowed and liberal congressmen voiced their approval as it made hefty annual payments to the United States treasury. No one in government complained that to make those payments whole communities of people and entire mountain ranges with their infinitely complex ecology had been sacrificed.

With TVA's insatiable demands for fuel the mountaineers learned anew the meaning of the old mineral deeds yellowing in courthouse vaults. Coal and its allies had no effective counterforce in Appalachian politics, and legislators and courts mirrored the industry's requirements. Obviously the land could not be stripped without destroying the surface, and more often than not the "surface estate" was owned by some mountaineer who naturally wished to preserve his land. After all, the old deed that bore his grandfather's X contained a covenant that the surface of the land was reserved to the grantor for such agricultural purposes as were not inconsistent with the right to mine. This produced a clash of interests, with coal winning every round in the contest. The courts ruled that the surface rights were "servient," so that the minerals could be extracted without any obligation to compensate the landowner for the ensuing ruin. Most mountaineers yielded complacently to these monstrous rulings, but some resisted, and in those cases there were armed deputies and state policemen to enforce the law. Explosions shook the hills, and during day and night roaring machines rushed the black lumps to the furnaces. While a number of new fortunes were being made by operators, the flow of uprooted people into Detroit and Hamilton quickened. As the destruction forced families out of the hollows to cluster in municipal housing projects and in trailer courts, the ancient social mores dissolved.

Since the rediscovery of the Appalachian dilemma a dozen years ago much has been written about the "colonialization" of the vast mineral fields and their exploitation by absentee landowners. In truth Appalachia was effectively converted into a raw-resource colony of the industrial North and West, and such families as the Fords, Mellons, Rockefellers, and Pews have greatly augmented their fortunes at the expense of this tormented region. One of Franklin D. Roosevelt's tasks after he left Harvard Law School was to abstract land titles in Appalachian courthouses for his uncle. His first trip to the hills was with his grandfather Delano, and much of the fortune that supported this "reformer" was drawn from coal veins in the Appalachians. Hundreds of billions of dollars worth of raw materials have been carted away from Appalachia to the factories of the world—timber, coal coke, talc, cement rock, clays, copper, iron ore, sand and gravel, limestone road aggregates, oil, and gas—in a sustained orgy of extraction that proves one point beyond cavil: the extraction of raw materials on however large a scale need not give rise to a viable economy and general prosperity. If it were otherwise, Kentucky mountaineers would rank near the top of America's personal income scale. That the industrialization of this huge inland backwater brought mainly deepening poverty and dejection amid stupendous enterprises can be laid in large measure to rich and distinguished gentlemen in paneled boardrooms in Philadelphia and New York. They decided to use the political and economic clout of their corporations to keep local taxes on their property at an absolute minimum. This policy has been faithfully adhered to since the first railroad spike was driven on the Big Sandy and has effectively blighted a dozen Kentucky counties.

Low taxes on mineral properties immediately brought similar minuscule levies on farms and private homes. The result was empty treasuries, shoddy schoolhouses, undereducated and embittered teachers, dismal roads, and grotesquely crude medical services and facilities. From these, in turn, sprang illiteracy, ill health, and shiftlessness in a cycle the coal kings willfully perpetuate to this day. This exploitation and ruination of mountain people as a deliberate policy, when constructive alternatives could have been quite as easily adopted and sustained, has never been relaxed. Among other grim legacies it has bequeathed the nation a hundred thousand dust-choked men whose pensioning is costing the Social Security Administration, rather than corporate treasuries, billions of dollars in disability benefits. It has bound the region to a unitary economy wholly dependent on coal, frightening away prospective employers who might otherwise have invested in wood-using factories or in chemical plants producing coal derivatives. This, in turn, has subjected the entire society to alternate economic booms and busts, with rather more of the latter than the former. It has continued to spur outmigration of the ambitious and discerning while discouraging emigrés from returning with city-learned skills and disciplines. It is certainly true that the splendid profits of Appalachian land and mining companies have left a hideous legacy of social, economic, and environmental wreckage in their wake. Appalachia's industrial managers have been as callous and greedy as Cecil Rhodes. Spanish conquistadores wringing gold and silver from Mexico were no more pitiless than the twentieth-century tycoons who have shredded Appalachia. The Spaniards learned better and eventually lessened their exactions, but our industrial conquistadores have demanded the utmost farthing through good times and bad, the New Deal, the Fair Deal, the Great Crusade, the New Frontier, the Great Society, and Watergate.

But Appalachia's absentee landlords have had many willing helpers within the region. Their greed has been more than matched by that of local entrepreneurs who were, and are, all too willing to plunder their homeland and impoverish their kinsmen for profit.

The lack of an Appalachian land epic made the hill people willing collaborators in the destruction of their own region. The "every man for himself and the devil take the hindmost" attitude spawned on the frontier and perpetuated as part of the folk culture in the Appalachian backwater admirably conditioned the stronger and more ambitious mountaineers to enter the mainstream of American capitalism. They did so with a vengeance, and the names most commonly associated with resource pillage and human debasement are native to the region, were educated in its schools, reflect its basic values and attitudes, and bear the imprint of its pioneer settlers.

When one encounters a coal camp of flimsiest shacks, where the water is drawn from wells polluted by reeking privies, and the streets and sidewalks are no more than expanses of cinders and mudholes, the owners are almost always local men and women. Where strip mining has most savagely flayed the hills and reclamation has been most reluctant and niggardly, the operator is almost always a native son. Where safety standards are lowest and accident rates are highest, the pit is usually owned by a self-made entrepreneur who began his mining career as a laborer at the coal face. When one studies the records in the offices of county tax commissioners, the operators who hand in the skimpiest inventories with the scantiest values are generally people with children in schools their taxes support. And when the legislature convenes, it is native mountaineers who drive their Cadillacs and Lincoln Continentals to Frankfort to voice the most vociferous objections to tax reform, mine-safety laws, and reclamation statutes. If the owners of Penn-Virginia Corporation, Kentucky River Coal, the Big Sandy Corporation, Ford Motor, the Mellon companies, Kycoga, and the American Association are unobtrusive in legislative halls and executive offices, it is because local people willingly and effectively carry their banner and serve their cause.

Nor have mountain people in general condemned such practices. On the contrary, the local citizen who has accumulated a fortune at the expense of land and people is generally respected. Often he is honored with public office or a party chairmanship. While it is surely true that exploiters have wracked the Appalachians, it is doubtful that any people ever collaborated more willingly in their own debasement and in creating the circumstances that forced so many of them out of their homeland.

The draining away of people left the old men and women stranded with few or no followers to look to them for advice. The ancient patriarchy saw its elders abandoned as the young and the middle-aged went in search of greener pastures. Men and women who would have been oracles consulted by scores of friends and descendants were left as old-age pensioners in valleys which suddenly fell silent. And the young, their conservatism little abated in their new surroundings, were stripped of the stabilizing influence of the old. For a generation they were alienated strangers in the cities that harbored them, yearning for their homeland, cut off by archaic cultural traits from the greater society about them, lacking the assurance afforded by education and broad experience, bewildered as only a conservative folk can be when caught up in a rapidly changing world. To many urban social scientists the Appalachian migrant became an un-flattering stereotype: a slack, stooped, ignorant, and shift-less hillbilly.

The highway and television gave him a tenuous and baffling hold on a new culture. In the years of the great outgoing, old cars were plentiful and cheap and the expatriates bought them. The ancient rattletraps con-veyed the migrants from northern cities to the hills and back again. In the cities they could not live without recourse to the comforting influence of the hills, nor could they live without wages from the urban assembly lines. Twenty deeply troubled years would pass before millions of uprooted Appalachian mountaineers would think of themselves as anything but "briars." In time new ties converted them into citizens of Michigan, Illinois, Indiana, and Ohio, but in the transition they endured all the anguish Oscar Handlin has attributed to the uprooted Europeans who once washed up on our shores. Alto-gether four million of these highland people were in-volved in a migration more vast than the tide that carried the Okies and Arkies into California. A million came from eastern Kentucky alone.

The generation of adjustment to great cities was not an unmixed woe. Many mountaineers moved with resolute-ness to secure places for themselves in a new order because, like the starving Irish and tormented Jews of earlier years, they knew there was no turning back. They remembered valleys washed to the bedrock, lean fields brown with broom grass, the bean kettle bubbling with what was often the only food. They remembered work whistles that did not blow and dejected men waiting in frayed clothes for an occasional day in the mines. And the ambitious fought for job, place, and status in the cities and succeeded remarkably well.

Today a Kentucky mountaineer supervises the tax records of the District of Columbia and another struggles to bring order to Washington's traffic snarl and provide the city with an efficient system of mass transit. Another was chief clerk of the Senate until his retirement a few years ago. Others are high-level executives of major corporations. A few years ago a hill man reached the presidency of J. C. Penney Company, and when the bankrupt Penn-Central Transportation Company was reorganized, a canny mountaineer from Hazard, Kentucky, was given the job of directing the rescue effort. For a time in the 1960s and early 1970s four men born and bred in the Kentucky hills sat as colleagues in the United States Senate representing four different states.

Lexington, Kentucky, was practically captured by mountaineers who moved with shrewdness and ruthlessness to take over the city's business life, including its banks, insurance companies, and shopping centers. People from quaintly named eastern valleys became judges, ward bosses, surgeons, lawyers for huge corporations. The old Lexingtonians awakened to find mountain people entrenched in the centers of power.

Other mountaineers became teachers, principals, and superintendents in a half-dozen states, filling vacancies emptied as natives moved into higher paying jobs and professions. A few years ago a study revealed that in Butler County, Ohio, men and women from the southern hills occupied 65 percent of all teaching positions. As one administrator observed, "Kentucky captured Ohio without firing a shot!"

One of Detroit's top industrialists, Lee Iaccoco, president of Ford Motor Company, once observed in a private conversation that the men from the Appalachian hills who entered the factories in the postwar years were in the main hardworking, ambitious, and eager for overtime. They provided his and other companies a generation of dependable and capable labor amid the screech and whine of assembly lines at tasks that must be among the world's dreariest and most monotonous ways of earning a living.

Another stream of people moving out of the hills were strip-mine operators who prospered as the region sank. They were versatile and adaptive, and as their fortunes grew these new rich took their families to the city lights, assumed seats on such bodies as university boards, contributed to party coffers, and became shapers of public affairs. Governors come and go and political organizations rise and fall, but the influence of coal and its allies is constant. That power finances winners and losers alike and has never been in surer hands than those who reorganized and revitalized the industry in the great coal depression of the 1950s.

But there were those who could not or would not leave, who could find no job in the mineral industries, who could not teach or enter any of the other professions. Perforce they turned to welfare or public assistance as a way of life and have adapted to it in a long span which now reaches out to embrace the third successive generation. The multilayered assistance programs pay the recipients just enough money to give them a tenuous hold on survival and to habituate its "beneficiaries," or victims, to the monthly check. It undermines ambition and takes men out of the job market because acceptance of a job that may prove uncertain will bring an end to a small but dependable PA check. But the coveted check is never enough to feed, clothe, and shelter adequately, so houses decay, clothing turns to tatters, food is the same uninspired grub, bodies are too infrequently washed. In countless highland homes there is no expectation except the monthly stipend, no purpose beyond survival from one day to the next. The unexpressed realization of personal uselessness feeds on itself and breeds surrender, despair, alcoholism, drug abuse, and ultimately shiftlessness. In Central Appalachia circumstances have combined to produce a paleface reservation as stultifying as any ever prepared by bungling federal bureaucrats for their red-skinned victims.

For four decades now government has been locked into the same ineffective remedies for Appalachian poverty. It began with the depression dole, and the handout has since taken many forms—checks for the indigent aged, dependent children, the blind, and the disabled. Now it includes medical and hospital care and state-paid lawyers to defend pauper malefactors. There are crews of workmen who repair the decayed homes of "clients." Food stamps serve as money to supply cut-rate groceries. These aids do nothing to instill self-respect in either old or young but leave the recipient to retreat to his trash-littered community to live a life nearly as individualistic and unrestrained as in the beginning. Assistance without corresponding duties in return has not worked, as relief rolls swollen in many counties to embrace a third of the inhabitants clearly disclose.

The situation that has evolved appears tailor-made ultimately to reduce the remaining human stock to genetic ruin. For nearly two centuries large families have increased the population so that from time to time there are huge outflows, and those who leave are the rebellious, intelligent, and ambitious. Those who persevere in the classroom until a high school diploma is achieved slip away with the dexterity of convicts escaping a prison farm. This ceaseless hemorrhaging of the best blood has already had a discernible effect. The deteriorating situation moved one wag to note that "the best thing the federal government could do for the mountains is to move a big army camp in. The soldiers would get the local girls pregnant and the fresh genes would do more good than all the free grub they're giving away." The observation evoked laughter seasoned with the realization that it contained more truth than wit.

# 4

# THE TRUTH
# THAT LIBERATES

THE MISSION SCHOOLS and church-supported colleges have educated countless youths who otherwise would have continued in the old rut of ignorance and poverty. In one respect, however, these schools, like the public schools, have been calamitous: they have educated their students for the outside world rather than for the building of prosperity and well-being at home. They have, as a rule, given a glimpse of distant urbia, and the graduates have taken their diplomas to areas already surfeited with the well trained while their homeland suffers from a chronic lack of educated brains. Schools at all levels have been guilty of a colossal failure in that they do not teach and have never taught fundamental truths about the Appalachian land: how misuse of the land has led to social and economic decline for most of the inhabitants, how exploitation of the land has built great fortunes for a few, how wise use of the land might make the word "Appalachia" a synonym for progress instead of blight. The hill people probably know as little about their native heath as any folk on earth, and for the dire consequences the schools must shoulder a major share of the responsibility.

In the main, mountaineers are blind to the geology of their region. People who have spent all their lives in the shadow of cliff-crested hills have no comprehension of the natural forces that created them. The fascinating aeons that raised the long ragged fracture that is Pine Mountain, the brooding immensity of Big Black Mountain, the finely textured, little-hill terrain of the Cumberland Plateau are total mysteries. Mysteries, too, are the vast and age-old processes that laid down the beds of coal, oil, gas, salt, iron, limestone, and silica. And since the highlanders have no understanding of the geology they cannot grasp the magnitude of the land's riches and the importance of those riches to the rest of the world. The geology of Appalachia is thoroughly documented and the lack of a general understanding of it reflects an appalling shortcoming on the part of the schools and their patrons.

Forests once cloaked Appalachia like the folds of a mighty carpet—a blend of interrelated and interdependent trees, vines, ferns, flowers, lichens, and grasses. In eastern Kentucky the deciduous American woodland achieved its climax, its fullest and finest expression. More than 2,000 flowering plants have been counted in the area; and there, ages ago, occurred the floral genesis that eventually clothed North America with timber and, in a period when the continent was linked to Asia, seeded colonies of its plants into the gentle hills of eastern China. At other times the inexorable ice-sheets shoved down most of the plant forms known to the northland, seeding them southward to the shoulders of the desolation for Appalachian seeds to cloak anew, southern plants crept northward and found their way into the same sheltering hills. In this way the Appalachians became the living repository of an incredible, and incredibly ancient, collection of plants gathered by nature's timeless forces from the Alaskan North Slope to Florida. Thus we can be intrigued to find an Alaskan rock lichen sheltering under a magnolia whose primordial ancestors grew by the sweltering Everglades. Kentucky's Red River Gorge is a marvelous showplace of this botanical museum.

The splendors of the forest were minutely catalogued nearly a half-century ago by Dr. E. Lucy Braun in her definitive treatise *The Deciduous Forests of Eastern North America*. The forest is approximately 50 million years old and its hard and soft woods, beautiful blossoms, and medicinal herbs are invaluable. Since the beginning of the settlements, fires, insect blights, ground clearings, mining, and numerous other activities have ravaged it on a gargantuan scale, but with the exception of the chestnut which disappeared before a deadly blight fifty years ago the seeds are still there. The rain still falls and the lands devastated by mining can, to an appreciable degree, again be made fit for trees. We have seen this occur in the old corn and pasture fields: first the frail seedlings a couple of inches high, then shoots springing in only a season or two to eye level, thence to sturdy saplings straining against one another in a struggle for precious sunlight. As the trees come back the branches and trunks of those doomed in the struggle join the annual rain of leaves and needles to form decaying compost. As this litter builds, something magical takes place: from sheltered nooks amid the ferny cliffs along the ridges seeds are washed and blown, and the old low-growing ground cover reappears. They come trooping back one by one and year after year to clothe the earth once scarred by axe and plow, huge foul-smelling skunk cabbages, obscenely rank mayapple, ginseng, yellowroot, jack-in-the-pulpit, ferns. These and scores of other plants form a subforest in the shade of the larger one rising above it. This woodland, so tenacious of life and so deeply rooted in the vicissitudes and triumphs of antiquity, is Appalachia's glory. Its walnut, maple, and oak are carried away to the furniture makers of Italy and to Japan's giant Yamaha piano factories. Its white oak mellows the wine and whiskey of two continents. Its substance is in the roofs and walls of our

*40*

houses. The drinking water of millions of people bubbles and trickles from amid its roots. Its fronds release oxygen into a world swathed in foul industrial gases. Here, struggling to survive and restore itself, is one of America's greatest assets, comparable in importance to the wheat fields of Kansas and the cornfields of Iowa. Incredibly, two centuries after the coming of Daniel Boone native mountaineers can think of nothing to do with it except to cut it down and ship it away to more ingenious and ambitious people.

Colleges, high schools, and elementary schools generally ignore the woodland, largely because their teachers know so little about it. Today a typical eastern Kentuckian cannot tell a black oak from a black gum or a hickory from a hornbeam. Though the people of China will pay more than sixty dollars for a pound of dried ginseng root most Kentuckians can walk past it without recognition. The furniture makers of Sorrento mortgage their homes, shops, and mills to buy cherry, walnut, maple, oak, and poplar wood of the kind Kentucky road builders daily send up in smoke! In our ignorance we blithely burn what they would turn to polished treasure. The Appalachian people will find little relief from their old poverty and backwardness until they understand this gigantic woodland and acquire the initiative and skills that will make its timber, beauty, and solitudes saleable on a self-renewing and perpetual basis.

The economics of Appalachia, like its geology and botany, remains an abiding riddle to the highlanders and their teachers. The region's mines, quarries, wells, and sawmills have generated immense fortunes and lined whole city blocks with mansions, but the mansions are not in the hills. The fortunes were amassed by means that rendered the country unfit for rich men to inhabit, so the rich moved away leaving the battered land to the poor. The landscape is dotted with signs bearing such names as Ashland Oil, Ford, Republic Steel, Bethlehem Steel, National Steel, United States Steel, A. T. Massey, International Harvester, Koppers Corporation, Occidental Petroleum, Inland Steel, Duke Power, Equitable Gas, and Georgia-Pacific. All are engaged in the business of hauling Appalachia away by the ton, barrel, or plank. All strive to capitalize Appalachia's profits while socializing its losses, as illustrated by the federal black-lung compensation law that pays miners compensation for illnesses sustained in the mines. All are enormously profitable, and all swell their profits at the expense of Appalachia.

The magnitude of these profits was pointed up a decade ago in an article published in *Dunn's Review and Modern Industry* in April 1965. The report described the Penn-Virginia Corporation as an obscure Appalachian land company that had acquired the distinction of being America's most profitable investor-owned corporation. Penn-Virginia was clearing after taxes 61 percent of gross receipts and was paying its stockholders 45 percent of all income. The main problem facing the company, according to its president, was "an embarrassment of riches." The article did mention, however, that in east Kentucky such companies are not rare. Kentucky River Coal Corporation, a neighbor to Penn-Virginia, was identified as the nation's number two profit-maker, in terms of percentage. By contrast, General Motors boasts when it clears 10 percent of gross and pays 5 percent of gross receipts to shareholders.

These two land companies and a score or more like them have enjoyed nine years of unprecedented prosperity since the article was published. In the meantime Perry County, Kentucky (where Kentucky River Coal earns the lion's share of its revenue) made the smallest contribution of any county in the state to the support of its school system, a mere 3 percent. In nearby Knott County a 14,000 acre tract of prime metallurgical coal was "developed" by a huge steel company at a cost of $15 million. The minerals that made it all possible paid the county a princely 23 cents per acre annually. High corporate profits and low corporate taxes at the local level continued to spawn those old, disparate twins: local poverty and distant wealth.

During the 1960s the Johnson administration grandiloquently declared a war on poverty and passed the Appalachian Redevelopment Act. The spotlight of national attention focused on the Kentucky hills and hundreds of millions of dollars were pumped in for highways, housing, job training, medical care, social security payments, and direct public assistance grants of many kinds. Through it all colleges and universities that serve the region unwittingly did their share to perpetuate the economic distress. None hired a professor to teach a course on the economics of the Appalachian region. All continued to spread the worn myth that Appalachian people are poor because their land is poor and, by implication at least, that the wisest course is to leave. Thus indifference on campuses combined with greed in boardrooms to work the ruin of one of the fairest and most promising parts of the globe.

West Virginia calls itself the Switzerland of America but the comparison is grotesque. The state could have been a new Switzerland if its inhabitants had possessed the leadership, wisdom, and ambition to take it along that kind of constructive road. But like their kinsmen in eastern Kentucky they chose to follow a different course, prompting Arnold Toynbee to write that in Appalachia is found the melancholy spectacle of a people who have "acquired civilization and then lost it." He writes that highlanders have reverted to "barbarism," becoming the "Rifis, Albanians, Kurds, Pathans and Hairy Ainus" of the New World. This blanket judgment is far too harsh, but it effectively points up the fact that we of the hills have in truth retreated from great possibilities and rejected great challenges.

A comparison of Switzerland with eastern Kentucky can be startling. It can help us to see the immense scale of

*43*

our lost opportunities and to discern with clarity what we might achieve for ourselves and our posterity if we undergo a constructive change of heart.

Switzerland, like eastern Kentucky, is mountainous. The territories are approximately the same size, each containing about 15,000 square miles. Each is in a heavily industrialized continent filled with highly competitive people. But here the similarities end and the astounding dissimilarities begin. The soil of Switzerland is poorly endowed. Twenty-one percent of it is utterly barren, permanently swathed in snow and ice. The steep slopes rise to prodigious heights where the air is thin and icy, and men can survive only by intense effort. The forests are sparse and limited in variety. The only mineral deposits of real significance are the brine beds which are pumped and used by the chemical industries.

The little country struggles beneath other burdens. For many centuries its large neighbors have been predatory, compelling the Swiss to maintain a huge military establishment. Road building is staggeringly expensive. To compound the difficulties the people are drawn from three distinct national backgrounds, each with its own language, prejudices, and mores. The schools teach all three tongues, Italian, French, and German, while large numbers of rural people speak an ancient fourth tongue, Romansch. The very survival of nationhood requires tact and forbearance by government and citizens alike. The country is landlocked and must haul every item it imports and each product it exports over another nation's roads and rails. By all reasonable standards Switzerland should have disappeared as a sovereign state, crumbling under the burdens of high taxes, foreign diplomatic entanglements, lack of foreign markets and exchange, overpopulation, shortages of wood and food, and internal dissensions.

A Kentuckian must smile when this geographical hopelessness is compared with the eastern third of his own state. The Kentucky hills are dark with forest, the infinite variety and potential of which have already been noted. After nearly six decades of intensive mining 35 billion tons of heat-rich coal remain untouched in the ground. A consortium of oil companies holds leases on a million acres of the "deep horizon"—strata which their geologists say are "very promising." An official document issued by the Department of the Interior in 1968, *The Mineral Resources of the Appalachian Region,* terms Appalachia one of the richest raw material regions on earth, and the Kentucky ridges are near its heart. Despite the scars of mining, including those gigantic lacerations sometimes referred to as the "scars of Bethlehem," there is still much breathtaking natural beauty. In a nation beset by a deepening water crisis these green hills count nearly fifty-five inches of precipitation a year. Its climate is equable and mild. Its bottomlands, impressive in scope along the Cumberland and Big Sandy rivers, are fertile and friable. In World War II the beleagured Swiss fed themselves on grain and potatoes from a far scantier land base. Truly this is a land nature smiled on and one would assume that here America would achieve its loftiest levels of general affluence and well-being.

But developments within these two mountainous territories have not come as one might have expected. The Swiss accomplishments have been incredible in their range and scope while we eastern Kentuckians have been monumental failures on our own turf.

One hundred and seventy-two years after their liberation from Napoleon the Swiss are bankers and insurance brokers on a worldwide scale. (My own home in the Appalachian heartland is insured by one of their companies.) Some twenty billion United States dollars are shepherded by their banks and only the West German mark compares with the Swiss franc for hardness and worldwide negotiability. The country supports twenty-two institutions of higher learning, including five top-quality medical schools. Illiteracy has been brought to what appears to be an irreducible minimum, less than 1 percent of all adults. Cleanliness and excellent public hygiene laws have made their health standards the envy of the world. Their magnificent armed forces guard the country effectively and efficiently, but without the panoply and vast expense of huge standing forces. The people work so industriously that the 5 million Swiss are insufficient to do all the needed tasks and 700,000 foreign laborers have been imported from larger and less sensible countries. The country's prosperity is awesome, reporting an official annual unemployment rate of about fifty people and, in some cities, one millionaire for each five hundred citizens. The president is elected for a one-year term, rides a streetcar to work each morning, pays out of his own pocket for any repairs that are made to his home, pays his taxes promptly and fully, tells the truth, and scrupulously avoids burglars, wiretappers, conspirators, and other people of low morals and ill repute. Consequently, the government is renowned for its honesty. America can learn a lot from the Swiss about how to make democracy work, beginning any time we are willing to take a serious look at their dynamic and effective example.

Kentucky mountaineers have been cursed by the riches of their land. For a few score thousand dollars they transferred legal title to them to "furriners," then routinely elected judges and legislators who steadfastly sided with the coal owners in all clashes between their rights and those of the resident population. These officials stood by while mining mangled mountains, ruined streams, and made broad areas into wastelands. They were slow to enact safety laws, then allowed the statutes to go unenforced while limbs were mangled, eyes were blinded, and lungs were choked with dust. The impoverished schools have left a fifth of the adults in illiteracy with the concomitant that a third are on relief.

Eastern Kentucky has been widely regarded as the nation's most somber rural slum, the "shame of a nation," as it was often called in the 1960s. Outmigration has reduced the populace to little more than a relief-support-ed remnant, considerably fewer than the 800,000 Italians, Yugoslavs, and Turks who now supplement the native Swiss labor force. So many people want to move to Switzerland that it is compelled to enforce the world's strictest immigration laws. Eastern Kentucky has long sustained the highest outflow of people in the Western world.

The Swiss mountaineers took a depressingly poor land and, by good judgment and hard work, became rich, powerful, and respected. Kentucky mountaineers took a rich land and became poor. The huge achievements in the Alps flow from a popular willingness to make hard decisions and to seize and carry through burdensome responsibilities. The resounding flop in the Appalachians reflects a historic abdication of responsibility to raise up stable leaders, to fashion sound public policies, and to implement them. In both situations what might be called "cultural determinism" was at work and still works to impel one people toward the heights and to sink the other into dependency and degradation.

How might the tragedies of the Appalachians have been avoided? Or, more aptly, how may the present mess be converted into a genuine North American Switzer-land? The answer lies in a change of attitude toward government and a willingness to use this prime tool for huge and constructive tasks. As long as Kentucky moun-taineers mistrust government, keep it weak, and elect jovial nonentities to govern them, they have no hope for significant social, moral, or political improvement. In Kentucky politics it has become a case of the bland leading the bland, with predictably bland results.

When Felix Schneider, the Swiss ambassador to the United States, visited eastern Kentucky in 1969 he saw schools, coal mines, and food stamp offices. After a thor-ough exposure to the Appalachian malaise, he was asked, "What can we do to make eastern Kentucky like Swit-zerland?" Without hesitation he replied, "All your problems are political. Adopt constructive political ideas and practices and your present troubles will disappear." Therein His Excellency the Ambassador laid his finger on the fateful genesis of our ills, born as they were in a long-ago flight to the backwoods in a vain attempt to elude the inescapable. The hard task of using government, in Abraham Lincoln's phrase, "to do for people those things that need to be done, but which the people acting by themselves cannot do," was shirked. In our postfrontier age of interdependence and accelerating homogeneity such an attitude is not only archaic but also deadly.

A foolish American myth has it that the rich and super-rich are entrepreneurial Daniel Boones who decry the restraints of government and, as rugged individualists, fare forth to wrest fame and fortune from other like-minded souls. With some notable exceptions nothing could be farther from the truth. In the main the rich are the clever and adroit who understand the purposes and functions of government and bend it to their purposes. Government becomes a device which they use to expand their fortunes, then hide behind to make certain their gains remain intact.

A prime illustration of government bent to serve the rich is, of course, the Internal Revenue Code with such provisions as its mineral depletion allowances, long-term investment credits, and tax exemptions for municipal bonds. Whatever the reasoning given to congressmen when the code was written and when it is occasionally amended and "reformed," the rich get richer, growing numbers of the poor drift onto relief rolls, and the middle class toil to preserve their status quo and pay most of the bills for the whole operation. Nor is this situation notably blameworthy, since the middle class have the numbers and power to correct the injustices and imbalances anytime they decide to bestir themselves to that end. Just as eternal vigilance is the price of liberty, eternal vigilance is the price of economic security. It is the price, too, of special privilege, a price America's rich have willingly paid. (The fall of Spiro Agnew illustrates what happens on those infrequent occasions when the rich get caught "influencing" a politician whom their money has cozened the unrich into electing.)

Appalachian mountain people were not vigilant when encroachments were made against the underpinnings of their independence. In 1884 the West Virginia Tax Commission surveyed the large-scale mineral purchases then being made in that state by absentee interests and issued a warning that should have been heeded throughout the entire mountain range. Unless people recognized that sovereignty was passing with the title deeds, the commission warned, and acted to keep landownership in local hands, all the abuses inherent in absentee landlordism would inevitably ensue. Then, the commissioners predicted, "the history of West Virginia will be as sad as that of Ireland and Poland."

The warning was ignored and the new landlords displayed the same cynical disregard for the native inhabitants that characterized Polish and Irish masters. In each situation the common people were abruptly rendered superfluous when the landowners adopted new tools and techniques that did not require their labor. In their time the Irish and Polish peasants fled to America, and in our time the Appalachian highlanders fled to other states. The Appalachian people did not starve to death as a million Irish did. The vast food stocks of the Department of Agriculture prevented that, but hundreds of thousands ceased to be relevant to the nation's life and became a kept people. History may record this as a form of death, at least in a societal sense.

No amount of relief, no number of helpful "programs" will produce major benefits unless a tremendous cultural upheaval takes place: wholesale abandonment of fear of government and the rise of a pragmatic realization that government is here to stay and must be used constructively for public gain. This would involve something totally different from the present passive reliance on government checks, food stamps, boxes of free food, "free" medical payments, and inconsequential jobs. It would mean the adoption of the practical wisdom of the wealthy by the general public—that numerous, sometimes faceless multitude known as the "men in the streets." If done after the Swiss fashion it would avoid the corruption that put free food and whiskey on Spiro Agnew's shelves and brought untallied millions into Richard Nixon's political treasury. It would have to be, as in Switzerland, a self-help, "made at home" operation because the federal government, responsive as it is to the huge interests that own the region, is unlikely ever to sponsor such developments.

I do not for one moment suppose that the grass-roots program of political and economic reform I am about to suggest, or any other major effort, will be undertaken within this century. Perhaps no comparable effort will ever be launched. The forces that support the status quo are formidable indeed, including immense transportation firms, fuel conglomerates, some of the nation's largest and most influential banks, and, of course, the legions of leashed and obedient politicians at all levels of government who do their bidding for pay. At this juncture in our history the American electorate appears too debased to give rise to great and effective leaders or to sustain and support them, and eastern Kentucky is no exception to this generalization. The people corrupt and degrade their leaders in the process of electing them, then their leaders corrupt and debase the people to gain their continuing approval. It is a continuous and ultimately ruinous cycle from which there is no present prospect of escape and which emphasizes at every turn the petty, the commonplace, and the mundane. In a nation whose ordinary political workings could generate the preposterous chicaneries of Watergate, few innovations can be expected to arise in what economists and sociologists have called its most backward region.

The Appalachian culture virtually rules out any grand scheme requiring broad points of view and keen insights. It is a culture that frowns on experimentation and chance-taking, the new, the risky, and, above all, the large. It is in the modern world that finances and manages vast global enterprises and explores the outermost reaches of the imagination, but it is not in a real, integral sense a part of that world. The inhibitions of an old, deeply rooted system of mores and values can curtail human achievement as effectively as walls or iron bars, and it is as unlikely that Kentucky mountaineers will, as a society, embrace the enterprise and ambition of the Swiss as it is that the people of that Alpine republic will lapse into poverty and welfarism. In each case supremely strong imperatives are at work of which neither people can be fully cognizant and from which neither can escape except by slow degrees and over a long time.

It does not harm to dream of remote possibilities, however. Appalachian Kentucky has turned much of its heritage and hope into ashes, but there remains a frail chance that the phoenix of greatness will be sparked by the expiring embers.

A glance at the manner in which the Swiss have managed their own affairs affords insights into some of the approaches they would employ, and we could employ. Their genius with government has enabled them to put large facets of their economy, including railroads, communications, electric power, and much of heavy industry in public ownership, while leaving to individuals and their private enterprise the broad variety of the nation's affairs, including farming, watchmaking, banking, retailing, innkeeping and, of course, their fabulous chocolate candy factories.

If we would emulate them our first step would be to place in public ownership the huge mineral resources of our eastern and southeastern counties. Title would not vest in the far-off federal government to be administered by an impersonal, unimaginative, and inflexible Bureau

51

of Land Management. The Swiss keep government visible and within manageable reach, and the Kentuckians would gain nothing by transferring their basic resources from investor-owned corporations to federally owned corporations. TVA has demonstrated that a government corporation can afflict a land and its people as grievously as any coal or steel corporation.

The Public Utility Districts of the State of Washington illustrate the type of locally managed governmental entity that Americans can employ to build a Swiss-style society in a fading rural backwater. They demonstrate, too, the kind of political reforms Ambassador Schneider may have had in mind when he remarked that all of our problems are political.

In much of Washington the principal natural resource is the abundant water flowing in the Columbia River. Twenty-five years ago big utility companies on the one hand and big government on the other were moving to seize the river's hydroelectric capacity. Whether the race was to be won by Puget Sound Power and Light Company or the Department of the Interior's Bureau of Reclamation would be of little consequence to the inhabitants. Neither of the would-be expropriators consulted the rate-paying public. The old American custom of snatching resources was being followed in the routine way by both sides.

Then suddenly something quite unexpected—and in a sense quite un-American—transpired. Some people discovered an old and neglected state-enabling statute and decided that the river should be used by and for the people of the counties through which it flows. The act had been passed years before and was aimed at getting electricity into widely scattered rural homes. It empowered the people of a district, ranging in size from a voting precinct up to a county or a combination of counties, to decide by a referendum to form a public corporation functioning as a utility district. A public utility district (PUD) so formed is governed by elected directors, has the power of eminent domain, and is authorized to raise capital by the sale of bonds. The directors are charged with the duty of providing ample electricity throughout the district and developing human and natural resources for the public welfare.

The events that ensued in Chelan County tell us what can happen when people elect sensible leaders and then employ government in a reasoned, prudent manner for public rather than private gain. At the PUD's inception the county had 40,000 inhabitants, fewer than Harlan County, Kentucky, at that time. Most of its land was cut-over, nearly worthless forest, and a part of it was semiarid. The lumber industry was a thing of the past and its main agricultural activity was apple growing. A long economic blight had drained away many people and it was gripped by depression.

If the county was to have a tolerable future, it had to be built on the electric power latent in the turbulent waters of the Columbia. The county undertook that task and in the face of stupendous difficulties succeeded beyond the wildest dreams of its planners. To most Americans, accustomed as they are to a dejected sense of local impotence and to waiting for federal funds and initiatives, the county's accomplishments in the last two decades seem unreal, impossible, even weird. To most people counties are anachronisms, holdovers from our simple agrarian past into an age of Big Government in Washington and fifty statehouses. The people of Chelan County brought their government to life, made its mechanisms work, gave the county a future where practically none was foreseeable, and provided people in other parts of the nation an object lesson in both democracy and economics.

The first things the new PUD and its president, Kirby Billingsley, did was to recapture a prime hydroelectric site from Puget Sound Power and Light Company. The corporation had built a low dam that developed only a portion of the river's immense capacity. Exercising its power of eminent domain the PUD condemned the existing facility, and after a lawsuit that eventually reached the United States Supreme Court, was ready to begin construction of its own plant. The Rocky Reach dam and generators cost somewhat more than $273 million, a tremendous outlay amounting to $6,800 for each of the county's inhabitants. In the years since this first successful venture into what might be called "people's capitalism," the PUD has spent another $228 million in supplemental installations, bringing the investment total to more than a half-billion. This stupendous project was financed by tax-exempt bonds of a kind investors eagerly seek and any county in the United States may, under proper conditions and safeguards, lawfully issue.

Power generated by the PUD is sold at wholesale to its old adversary, Puget Sound Power and Light, and to other utility companies, municipalities, and rural electric cooperatives. These, in turn, sell at retail to their numerous customers. A reliable and huge energy source was thus assured for the benefit of the entire region while the legitimate interests and profits of all parties were protected.

The predictable happened. The cheap electricity acted as a magnet to attract aluminum companies and a growing assortment of light industries. The payrolls stopped the outflow of people and caused newcomers to move in from the cities. Property values went up and, with them, the tax base. The county rose like a Lazarus pulling itself up by its own bootstraps to escape the fate of becoming a West Coast Appalachia-style rural slum. The PUD sells more than $28 million worth of electricity annually, three-fourths of which goes into a sinking fund to retire the bonded indebtedness. Most of the remaining $7 million is available for facilities and services to enhance the quality of life in Chelan County: schools, scholarships, hospitals, health services, libraries, reform-station projects, anticrime measures, grants to municipalities and the general county treasury. These funds have exerted a benevolent effect that is turning the county green again, putting factories in preplanned industrial parks, dramatically raising educational and vocational skill levels, and giving the area a sturdy reputation as a good place in which to live. In the near future all the bonds will have been retired. The debt-free district will then look to the river where $28 million each year will pour into the treasury with the foaming water roaring through the flumes—public funds, belonging to the people collectively and to be spent for their betterment as they direct. It may be said that local people arrested these funds for themselves and their neighbors, rather than allowing them to be siphoned off to the East Coast to the treasury of a giant electric power company.

Such lessons are not without meaning for Kentuckians. We could use the devices pioneered in Washington to solve many of our most pressing problems, provided, of course, that we decide we really want to solve them and become progressive enough to do so. Eastern Kentucky's resources are so huge by comparison that we could vastly exceed the impressive achievements of Chelan, Grant, and other Washington counties and their public utility districts.

Let us suppose for a fantastic moment or two that a progressive governor and legislature will decide to create an Eastern Kentucky Development District (EKDD) embracing all of our eastern hill country. The EKDD will be given powers like those of the West Coast PUD's and will be charged with the duty to catalog all the human and material resources of the territory. Its directors will be young, energetic, well educated, progressive, and without fear of man or Mellon. They will be mandated to use the natural resources to educate the people and to build an economic and social structure as prosperous and effective as any in the world. EKDD will aim, above all else, at wiping out the grinding poverty that has so long disgraced the region, ending the calamitous dependence on the dole, and bringing social and economic justice to a people who have become virtual outcasts from the centers of power in their homeland.

A spokesman for the same brokerage firm that sold Chelan County's bonds has estimated that EKDD could eventually raise $5 billion for the region's rehabilitation, and the first of such funds should buy—by condemnation, if necessary—the mineral resources of the region. The owners have stated under oath in the offices of the county tax commissioners what these minerals are worth, though to be candid it is likely that these stated values are at least a wee bit low. Fair prices should be paid and legal title to minerals between the tree roots and the "center of the earth" should vest in the developmental corporation.

EKDD will then decree that the coal and other substances will be extracted from the earth in such a manner as to minimize damage to streams and forests. Aesthetic considerations will be deemed of high importance and in those areas set aside for population centers, extractive activities will be prohibited altogether. The private-enterprise notion that land can rightly be put to death for all time for a single product useful only to this time will be discarded. It has already brought too much woe to the hills.

The agency's dams will impound water in multipurpose reservoirs and, unlike the Corps of Engineers, the agency will protect the lakes from degradation. Near them cooling towers and steam plants will rise, and Appalachia's colossal power potential will begin flowing into the nation's energy system. The latest and best technology will be installed throughout to hold air and thermal pollution to the lowest attainable levels. The profits now being reaped from eastern Kentucky coal will begin accumulating in the agency's accounts in mountain banks. Within a few years the miracle of Chelan County will begin to occur in the Appalachian heartland with dramatically far-reaching effects.

The availability and abundance of relatively low-priced power will attract new industries to Pineville, Harlan, Whitesburg, Hazard, Jackson, Prestonsburg, Salyersville, and Pikeville, ending the sick unitary economy so long dependent on the vagaries of the coal market. The immense demands for electricity—a finished product instead of a raw one—will stabilize the steam coal market and bring a new dimension of prosperity to the operators working as licensees in EKDD's coal veins, a prosperity their miners too will find exceedingly agreeable. In the veins primarily suitable for metallurgical purposes, minions of the great steel corporations will learn that they are no longer undisputed lords of the earth but must mine as if they possessed a social conscience.

Other effects are foreseeable. Funds from electricity sales and mineral royalties will finance industrial parks for chemical corporations using petroleum, gas, and coal. Crews of men will be set to work improving timber stands, clearing away the accumulated debris of the old coal industry, and revegetating "orphan banks" left by strip miners. Other funds will expand the schools to embrace kindergartens, modernize and enrich curricula, and build, perhaps at Prestonsburg, a genuine university with colleges of engineering, law, pharmacy, and medicine. Within a score of years the economic ripples emanating from such wise uses of minerals, plus a revivified forest-products industry and modernized agriculture will call forth the outlines of a totally new economic and social structure, a structure that will tend toward the wealth, stability, and self-confidence of Switzerland.

Nor are these grand visions beyond the reach of Appalachian Kentucky's resource base. The resources are there—charted, indexed, mapped, measured, and, by those who study such things, fully understood. The potential is there in the water, the plants, the green open spaces, the natural beauty, the coal, the oil and gas, the brines, the limestone, and the soil. The pipelines that lace the land and the rumbling coal "drags" are testimony to the ample riches of the land base. They testify, too, to the utter futility of great natural wealth where the people are poor in spirit and imagination and conditioned to an acceptance of low standards and aspirations.

Today's Kentucky mountain people are a pathetic remnant of the race that inhabited the hills four decades ago. The massive outflow of virile people has sapped and vitiated the human stock in much the same manner Portugal was drained and weakened by the long movement of people westward to Brazil. That population shift required centuries and left a once mighty nation—heir to half the world—a shrunken ministate, impoverished, sleepy, backward-looking, unimportant. The same circumstances have been at work in Kentucky's eastern counties, but the relative ease of traveling to the new El Dorados has achieved its sad result in little more than a generation. Eastern Kentucky's probable future can be visited today in Hawkins and Hancock counties in Tennessee, where almost total ruin has already been achieved. Its possible future can be visited in the bustling cantons of the Swiss Republic. The broad eastern third of the state will become a permanent wasteland, characterized by ever-deepening passivity and distress, unless the urban areas develop a sense of stewardship over it. The power of government is now effectively concentrated in Louisville, Lexington, and a few other cities, and in them are found the most talented and energetic of the state's people. Their prosperity cannot continue unless the hills prosper too, anymore than the great ballroom of a ship can remain happy once the bottom has dropped out. All Kentuckians are locked together in a single boat and every part should pull its fair share of the load. Perhaps the new generation of discerning politicians now surfacing in the cities will forge a fresh policy for the hills, a policy aimed at putting the region's resources to work for all the Commonwealth's people. They may be able to see before it is too late that as things now stand the eastern counties are a greater burden than the urban centers can carry, that ultimately high taxes and unmet local needs will sink the cities without saving the highlands. It is possible that the imperative of self-preservation will drive the cities to develop an urban stewardship of the state's land calculated to save the hills and, in the process, themselves.

The state's ancient sectionalism has traditionally left each region practically oblivious to developments in, and the needs of, other sections. This has left the rich mineral fields of east and west open to plunder by absentee corporations while uncomprehending urban taxpayers picked up the bill for the wreckage. This ignorant sectionalism has cost Louisville, for example, dearly indeed. Wealthy Louisvillians had no idea of what was afoot when astute traders from New York, Philadelphia, Baltimore, and London were acquiring title to eastern Kentucky riches worth many billions. These goodies were snatched from beneath their noses simply because Louisvillians with money to invest knew little about their own state.

There are unmistakable signs that this old ignorance is dissolving. House Speaker Norbert Blume of Louisville and former Governor Wendell Ford of Owensboro combined to push a coal severance tax through the General Assembly in 1972, a measure sixty years overdue and wholly unthinkable while the state was dominated by ultraconservative rural interests. The state's most vocal environmentalists live in its cities and champion streams and hills far from their own streets. Slowly but perceptibly the state is developing an awareness of its oneness, its inseparability, a development with truly revolutionary implications for everyone and everyplace from Mills Point to the Breaks of Big Sandy.

Nearly one-third of the money spent by Kentucky each year is raised in Jefferson County, another third reaches the state in the form of federal grants, and the balance comes from the remaining 119 counties. But, ironically, Jefferson County makes such massive contributions to the state coffers that it stays mired deep in fiscal crisis, with some of its schools on double shifts and threatened with forced retrenchments. Under the system imposed by existing law, schools in Kentucky's richest county will close their doors for lack of funds long before this dire eventuality comes to either Perry or Menifee.

If urban Kentuckians come to a real comprehension of the facts of life in their state, it is certain to compel drastic reforms in the school system. It may result in a common-sense work-and-learn approach like the one that succeeds so well in Switzerland. Those practical people send their children to school from 8:00 A.M. to 12:30 P.M., then they go home for lunch and spend the rest of the day studying or helping their parents on the farms and in the shops. Such wisdom saves the government the cost of elaborate school cafeterias and has practically eliminated juvenile delinquency.

All of this brings us back to James Madison's wise observation. Knowledge does indeed govern ignorance, and people who know the Kentucky land dominate the state while people who have never taken the trouble to understand it pay the taxes. The real masters of this Commonwealth sit in the boardrooms of huge coal, steel, oil, gas, rail, and chemical corporations. The regulatory and police agencies at Frankfort do their bidding as witnessed by their woeful efforts to enforce coal-trucking and land-reclamation laws. For the State of Kentucky to hit Bethlehem Steel Corporation with a "cease and desist" order is comparable to striking a tiger with a wet cornstalk. Neither the cornstalk nor the state agency has any backbone. The latter is a laughingstock because public apathy and ignorance make it operate without support from the people it "serves" while encountering brutal opposition from the people it "regulates."

If "popular information" is to dispel the tragedy of eastern Kentucky's poverty, backwardness, and human and environmental degradation, we must become realists with both feet firmly on the ground, as our Swiss mentors did long ago. Then in our schools, colleges, universities, offices, churches, and other organizations we must learn the facts that can set us free. We must know the geology, the botany, and the biology of our state's natural systems and the economics by which its resources have been used. We must learn where fortunes have been made from our land, and how and why, as well as the magnitude and the owners of those fortunes. We must learn, too, who has been sickened, maimed, and impoverished in the building of those fortunes, where they live, and by what means they now subsist. We must learn that nothing is permanent except change, and that alternatives can be found to the unsuccessful and the unjust. We must use such knowledge constructively, realizing that in these trying times Americans can no longer afford pockets of poverty and backwardness or be bound to pay the world's costliest electricity bills. We must shuck off forever that disgraceful old slogan "Thank God for Arkansas!"

# 5

# ON THE
# TIDES OF CHANGE

ARNOLD TOYNBEE has written that the Appalachian highlanders are the Western world's prime example of a people who faced a great challenge and surrendered to it. He may be right, but it is not too late to turn back and face the old challenge again, this time with new resolve and fresh insights. If we do rise to that challenge and enlarge our aspirations the mountain may come to Mahomet after all. In our own time, or soon thereafter, Swiss tourists may hike through our Appalachian woodlands and Swiss industrialists may maintain accounts in famous banks not far from Crummies Creek, Kingdom Come, War Branch, the Bull Hole, and Troublesome.

In recent years "futurists" have blossomed on the nation's campuses, latter-day seers who use accumulations of statistical data and studies of established trends to discern, as they believe, the shape of coming decades. Time and tide bring countless surprises and he is a brave man who assumes the role of prophet, whether his divinations emanate from a glass ball or from IBM's latest computer. But it is a truism that coming events cast their shadows before them and one can perhaps be pardoned for commenting on some of today's shadows and the upheavals they may portend.

Barbara Tuchman has noted that human institutions are sometimes least secure at the very time when they appear most unassailable. As examples, she cites the ancient, prosperous, and heavily armed empires of central and eastern Europe in 1914. By the end of 1918 their thrones had toppled, their armies had melted away, and men of whom the emperors had never heard were running the realms as presidents, chairmen, ministers, and commissars. Similarly, it may prove that in the 1970s America's vast corporations, foundations, and other capitalistic institutions, outwardly so serene and unshakable, were on a collision course with Cataclysm.

That enormously disruptive forces have become firmly stitched into the essential fabric of our society can no longer be denied. These forces are not new to human experience. To the contrary they have surfaced many times in the history of earlier societies and civilizations, and always they have produced revolutionary changes. They induce irresistible popular discontents, break down existing institutions and mores, and ultimately shift decisive power levers from old established blocs to clamorous new segments of the population. It would be foolish to predict such sweeping changes in American life, but it is equally silly to ignore the implications of the squiggles now etching themselves on our national seismographic charts.

The first of these forces dates back to World War II and the emergence of the United States as a military superpower. It is our immense military and naval apparatus and the endless wars that such power inevitably generates. Wars and preparations for wars drain off money that is desperately needed to satisfy the basic aspirations of impoverished millions. They produce recurring crops of embittered and rejected war veterans and necessitate tremendous systems of hospitals, elaborate and crushingly expensive pensioning arrangements, and unbelievably costly schemes for the retirement of numerous superannuated warriors. Despite the ado about détente there is no indication that this military monster can be gotten off our necks. The grim predictions of George Washington concerning the danger of a huge standing army are materializing before our eyes.

The second revolutionary force is the worldwide shortage of raw materials that has begun to engulf all countries. There appears to be enough coal and oil for the next several decades, but other supplies are running out. Copper, lead, tin, mercury, phosphate rock, natural gas, lumber and pulp, and many basic foods are already in short supply. The world population grows about 70 million per year and its demands for products rise even faster than its numbers. We are already in the first throes of a global scramble to find raw materials for factories and mills, and to clothe, feed, house, transport, and entertain multitudes already more numerous than earth can maintain at a bearable level. This scramble will lead directly to rearmament everywhere, the forging of military alliances, and, almost certainly, huge new conflicts. These tensions will produce ever-larger military outlays to exacerbate still further society's instabilities and tensions.

The third factor grows naturally and like some rank and hideous weed out of the other two. As we import more and more raw materials—of which petroleum and iron ore are only the most glaring examples—we will surely lapse again into chronic foreign exchange deficits. Our thirst for oil can pile up the wealth of the world in Arabia (unless those expensive military machines are used to seize the oil fields). We are dependent on the rest of the world for so much that two currency devaluations have been forced upon us within three years. Thus the nation Lyndon B. Johnson called "the richest and most powerful country in the history of the World" has seen its old independence drain away. It has watched money speculators in Switzerland, Germany, and Saudi Arabia drive the dollar to the brink of collapse, compelling our government to adopt fiscal and monetary policies it had repeatedly forsworn. The realization that the dollar is only as solid as our foreign trading partners allow it to be has already siphoned much of the arrogance out of our national character.

The fourth item on our ominous list is inflation. A vast military establishment, chronic shortages of raw materials, and international exchange deficits stimulate price rises on a horrendous scale. Day by day prices climb for fuel, food, clothing, and finished products. Workers and shareholders demand more income to meet the astronomical living costs, only to find the new dollars to be even more insubstantial than the old. People on fixed incomes are forced into starvation, respectable retired people are "inflated" into poverty. Labor unrest mounts as people struggle to buy bread, then discover that foreigners loaded with dollars from our huge payments deficits have already bought most of our wheat, corn, soybeans, lumber, salmon, and meat. In disgust and weariness multitudes quit work and "retire" or go on relief, adding by their idleness to rising costs and taxes and ever-higher prices.

A fifth demon haunts us, but it is a new one with which no earlier society has ever dealt. It is the combination of longevity and the birth control pill, an ill-assorted pair that prolongs the breath of millions of dependent people far beyond three score and ten years while drying up the supply of sturdy, hardworking taxpayers who must support them. This circumstance has stranded millions in scattered Appalachian shanties, in mansions along quiet shaded streets, in tiny cluttered rooms in decaying hotels, in "sun cities" designed especially for the old, in perpetual-care nursing homes, and finally in dead-end geriatric wards. Simultaneously young schoolteachers lose jobs as the flow of children dwindles and zero population growth looms—in the United States, at least—on the visible horizon. Social Security exactions rise as the helpless myriads multiply. Here is a ticking time bomb today's statesmen ignore but which another decade will build to gargantuan dimensions. Something will have to give:

either a lessening of our humaneness or a sharp decline in living standards for the working men and women throughout the land; even more likely, both will give.

In these matters we are dealing with nothing less than the ruination of the middle class and a surrender of America's much-vaunted "way of life"—a severely traumatic experience indeed, and one likely to produce what Spiro Agnew, in one of his more cogent interludes, once called "an uprisal and an overthrowal." Such problems must be dealt with by governmental policies and actions, but they converge on us at a time when popular confidence in government is at an all-time low. Watergate has brought to the surface for all to see and smell the massive, swelling corruption that has characterized our government for a century. Corrupt businessmen have worked with corrupt politicians to debase government, making it ludicrous and contemptible—scarcely a fit tool for coping with mammoth problems.

In any event, government efforts to alleviate social strains produce enormous new tax levies and staggering budgetary shortfalls. These, in turn, further debase money as a medium of exchange, forcing a return to barter and hopelessly complicating the mechanisms of trade. Already the Arab countries are demanding French weapons, factories, and other hardware in exchange for oil, and the Japanese rush to sign similar contracts to exchange manufactured goods for raw materials. Discerning people around the world stare into the yawning pit of monetary debacle and demand for their products something less ephemeral than engraved notes, bonds, and currency certificates.

But notes, bonds, and currency certificates are the lifeblood of our capitalistic system. If they lose their viability and universal acceptability the capitalistic system in America and abroad cannot survive. Like the *Titanic* grinding against the iceberg, it must sink. Thus it appears arguable, at least, that the architects and directors of our present system have set it upon a course that dooms it, in the not-far-distant future, to crack-up and dissolution.

The United States came to a comparable impasse in 1932. That crunch grew out of superabundance and underconsumption. Then a great, versatile, and imaginative conservative reached the White House in time to patch up a series of compromises that saved the old order. Today's assortment of Humphrey, Nixon, McGovern, Agnew, Eagleton, Ford, Kennedy, and Rockefeller afford scant hope, reminding us of "Happy" Chandler's marvelous asseveration that in Washington a man can get by without "guts, back-bone or brains!" The ship of state steams toward the iceberg and, as with Captain Smith on the *Titanic*, the skippers are employed elsewhere, largely in pursuit of tax dodges and private gain.

The young men and women of America who may have to reassemble the debris into some form of workable order will do well to ask themselves: Can a system of politics and economics that went from George Washington and John Adams to Richard Nixon and Spiro Agnew in less than two centuries find a means of saving itself?

The question seems to provide its own answer in the form of a sobering "no," which in turn will bring us face to face with the most momentous decisions confronted by the American people since the adoption of the Constitution.

It seems likely, then, that the nation is approaching a great watershed in its history when its priorities, values, and goals will have to be reassessed and drastic changes made in the ownership and use of land, water, air, topsoils, open space, scenic beauty, forests, and minerals. The states lying wholly or partly within Appalachia will have to come to grips with these questions and issues, for if the old arrangement breaks down it will scarcely be possible to put it together again, and as a return to the ancient regime will prove both undesirable and impossible, so avoidance of Soviet-style communism and bland and shaky English-style socialism will be equally imperative. Such a transition implies a long interval of turmoil and a determination that never again shall a small "generation of people" (to use an Appalachian expression), such as the Mellons, be allowed to own $6 billion worth of the country's basic wealth.

More than a quarter of a century ago in another time of great stress and uncertainty, Franklin D. Roosevelt declared, "This generation has a rendezvous with destiny!" The same may be said in an even more profound sense of the generation of Americans who will live out the middle age of their lives between now and the beginning of the twenty-first century.

The decisions made by those men and women will drastically affect the forested, rain-washed, mineral-rich Appalachian hills and the people who inhabit them. I envy all who shall live through those decisive and tumultuous years and participate, for good or ill, in the formulating of that future which at this moment cannot be even faintly glimpsed.

# 6

# NO EXCUSE
# FOR FAILURE

IN OTHER YEARS Kentucky and its highland people could offer plausible sounding excuses for the backwardness of the Cumberlands. It was said that the region lacked arterial highways and the state lacked funds to build them. Schoolhouses were few and inadequate, and there were not enough teachers. Isolation had generated such palpable ignorance as to make the population immovable. Too many people and an unregenerative agriculture bound them to rural poverty and made sound land use impossible. There was so much hardwood timber in America that the eastern Kentucky lumber markets were doomed to perpetual depression. The coal industry was so fragmented and its market so surfeited that the industry had to be nursed along, spewing out problems by every creek but providing no funding for solutions. The underfinanced and timid colleges and universities had little knowledge of the hills and lacked both the audacity and the resources to propose reforms. Besides, colleges were traditionally suspect as centers of radicalism where both communism and evolution were studied.

But as Kentucky comes to the end of its second century such excuses, and others like them, have lost their validity. Growing population in America and around the world,

69

global industrialization, and other significant changes wrought by the last two decades have created a drastically altered situation and, for all practical purposes, a new eastern Kentucky. With the old justifications and explanations gone we will have to shed our ancient self-image of backwardness, ill health, and poverty in a surge of reconstructive change, or continue in the old ruts under a new set of excuses. At the very least our spokesmen will have to bestir themselves to find additional explanations for the 1980s and 1990s.

In the last fifteen years state and federal efforts have given the mountains a system of decently designed and sturdily built arterial highways in lieu of the endless curves and shoulderless, unfenced tangles of KY 15, KY 89, and U.S. 119. The sales taxes and the Minimum Foundation Act have closed virtually all the high-perched, icy one-room schools, and in their stead have raised consolidated affairs earlier generations would have deemed palatial. The "emergency" nondegree teachers disappeared with the one-room schools and the shortcomings of the new pedagogues must be attributed to the colleges that trained them. The farmers have died or moved away to work on assembly lines at Louisville or in Detroit, and the millions of acres once given to sheep and cattle and the probing points of bull-tongue plows have gone back to splendid new forest. The fantastic growth of world markets has implanted sturdy new underpinnings in the coal and lumber markets. The banks in Pikeville finished 1974 with $290 million in deposits, an eloquent reflection of the new prosperity Time's unpredictable vicissitudes have brought to the hills. The 1975 election demonstrated that coal has measured its strength and desires to call the tune in the state's affairs. In Pike County alone coal operators and their friends raised nearly a half-million dollars to finance the bid of a favorite son for the lieutenant governor's office. Though he did not win he performed well, and the precedent was established. Kentucky now produces more coal than any other state, and the industry is the state's largest by any measure. The black lumps and the men who mine them will decide the shape of the future. In the new era the bourbon barons, the tobacco tycoons, and the genteel Bluegrass aristocrats will play second fiddle in an orchestra directed by King Coal. Precisely where this will lead us depends, of course, on just how the rest of the people—the one-gallus homemakers and taxpayers—react to the new order and the course they decide to set for themselves.

The year 1974 marked a watershed in the checkered story of the Kentucky mountains. The nation generally knew it as a year of recession and gloom in which unemployment rolls steadily lengthened, bankruptcies soared, and manufacturers closed their doors or curtailed production. Throughout the world inflation sapped savings and lowered standards of living, but the hills throbbed in a boom that caused jokesters to call the coalfield "little Arabia." Often in bust while the rest of the country boomed, the reverse was true in the bonanza year.

The boom sprang in part from panic induced by the sievelike oil embargo decreed by the Middle East states in the fall of 1973 and in part from the frantic efforts of steel and power companies to build stockpiles in anticipation of a prolonged miners' strike at the expiration of the labor contract in November 1974. It grew, also, out of a switch from oil-burning utilities back to coal and, most importantly perhaps, out of news media blatherings about a permanent "energy crisis." These stimulants evaporated when the United Mine Workers of America signed a contract after a brief work stoppage and the State Department modified its "principles" sufficiently to mollify the Arabs. As the world boom subsided like a leaky tire, demands for energy declined and suddenly there was an abundance again, but at prices elevated to reflect reams of printing-press money spawned by repeated federal deficits. However, in a profounder sense the Appalachian coal boom was born of much more enduring factors: a world population of four billion and enormously enlarged individual aspirations. Thus while the boom sagged with the end of the bonanza year, it did not collapse but continues to grind out millionaires—though at a slower rate.

The bonanza year began with the oil embargo and a floundering president's plans to deal with it, and extended for a full twelve months to the middle of November 1974. The beginning of 1973 saw the eastern Kentucky coal industry in the doldrums, its product selling for eight or nine dollars per ton. Tied largely to the hectic and uncertain "spot order" market most operators were pessimistic about the future. Their lack of long-term sales contracts became their good fortune when foreign and domestic steel makers and coal-hungry utilities suddenly realized that coal stocks were short, the oil tankers might cease to run for a while, and miners might cease to work. Steel production and consumption were at all-time highs despite the impending recession—and they, too, rushed to buy coal. Most large operations were bound by long-term contracts, so the uncommitted spot operations churned into action to meet the frenzied new demand. As purchasers bid against one another, prices soared so that by the autumn of 1974 quantities of top-quality metallurgical fuel were selling for as much as ninety dollars to the ton. This stupendous price run-up vastly exceeded wage and supply cost increases and left the spot market suppliers reveling in great gobs of cash.

It was not uncommon for a man with a tiny mine and a half-dozen employees to net five or six thousand dollars weekly. Larger operators did far better and men with docks to load their output into railroad cars could clear twenty to fifty dollars per ton. Strippers removing mountaintops were sometimes even more prosperous because their production costs were rarely more than half those of underground pits. Bank deposits swelled in a severe case of financial elephantiasis, and bond and stock brokers in

72

Lexington and Louisville were assigned the pleasant tasks of investing the money for their newly rich customers. Some brokers had clients who tucked away from ten to twenty-five thousand dollars daily in this manner. Real estate dealers saw opportunities in the hills and coal money began acquiring Bluegrass farms in a half-dozen counties.

The hills blossomed with expensive new homes ringing the county seats and sprawling along the strips of bottomland and raw, 'dozer-gouged terraces on the hillsides. The coal boom was enlarged by an eruption of "black lung money" pouring out of Washington as belated compensation to thousands of disabled miners. Simultaneously another significant flow of cash came from the welfare and retirement fund of the United Mine Workers as federal courts required the pensioning in eastern Kentucky alone of five thousand previously rejected claims. These outpourings mingled to spread in all directions to the enrichment of doctors, dentists, lawyers, merchants, automobile dealers, and, by no means least, the vendors of mobile homes.

The ancient, rust-eaten, smoky junkers that had so long symbolized the Appalachian coalfields went to the scrap yards or piled up in forsaken strings along roadsides. New cars multiplied like locusts in the seventeenth year and scores of Cadillacs, Continentals, Mercedes, and a few Rolls Royces mingled with the immense Mack, Ford, and Peterbilt coal trucks. In home construction and car buying, the hills ran directly contrary to national trends as most Americans slowed down and retrenched.

The most spectacular change wrought by the bonanza year was in housing. Unable to obtain builders within the hills, shocked by the stratospheric cost of conventional homes, and enticed by the immediate availability of house trailers, the newly prosperous turned to these units on an incredible scale. By the hundreds and then by thousands they came in over the new parkways and turnpikes—gaudy, ugly, and flimsy, but cozily convenient. The old camp houses, the three- and four-room shacks along the creeks, and the frail, rough shotgun shelters bequeathed by the lumber booms had decayed for generations, and now they disappeared to make room for the metal-shod, even more frail rectangles. Hooked to deep wells and septic tanks, air-conditioned and electrically heated, the mobiles brought an immense, almost instantaneous, enhancement of housing and living standards.

They also bound their new owners to long years of high-interest installment payments and created a certainty that at some time in the future the region will have to cope with an unimaginable junk problem as entire communities of the boxes reach the end of their usefulness. The pileup of worn-out cars has presented difficulties that enormous increases in scrap prices and innumerable clean-up campaigns have done little to mitigate. The junking of nearly as many of these small instant houses will try the ingenuity of the 1990s. Notwithstanding their obvious shortcomings it cannot be denied that the mobile homes are infinitely better than the shelter most of the people had previously experienced and are greater in their volume than all the housing raised by the camp builders in the industry's greatest decades.

The bonanza year ended, as all booms do, and for some producers few orders came after mid-November 1974. But despite the nation's worst recession in thirty years and a rash of bankruptcies in many industries, coal did not collapse. The prices declined but not to their levels at the beginning of the boom. It is significant for the future that demand stabilized and prices held at nearly double those prevailing two years before. In 1948 coal collapsed while the national economy soared. In 1975 coal prospered amid a nationwide near panic. This portends Appalachian coal booms when a general recovery begins.

There can be no certainty that a severe, bone-jarring coal depression will not come again to the hills. International currency troubles or runaway inflation are only a couple of circumstances that could dry up world trade and eventually send the prices of all commodities, including coal, into a dizzying plunge. In today's context ten-dollar coal would spell disaster of the kind that came with three-dollar coal in the 1950s. Such prices would bring a rerun of those grim days with mass bankruptcies, receiverships, ex-tycoons reduced to ragged clothes and rattletrap cars, miners shoved again into relief lines, and new waves of outmigration. Like coffee in Brazil, there is an awful lot of coal in the United States, and we know from bitter experience that gluts can build up with shattering speed. But the Federal Energy Administration has calculated that Kentucky's production of the fuel will increase 49 percent in less than a decade, an estimate knowledgeable state officials and some coal operators consider very conservative.

As this is written the spot market is sliding into a new stretch of hard times that will doubtless eliminate many poorly financed, fly-by-night operators. Since such companies can survive only through harsh and unrelenting exploitation of land and people, little will be lost to the state if they go by the board.

Despite the difficulties of the spot-market suppliers there are signs that eastern Kentucky coal has entered an era of reshaping and of formidable prosperity. The territory's huge coal veins are being inextricably tied to and appropriated by vast international steel and energy agglomerations that think and plan in terms of decades, covenant with governments as well as with other corporations, and avoid the vagaries of the spot-order business as they would the plague.

The recasting of the region's major industry is being brought about this time by subsidiaries of big oil, applying many of the techniques learned in supranational petroleum trading. Ashland Oil has huge coal operations in the hills. Armand Hammer's immense Occidental Petroleum owns Island Creek Coal, one of the state's largest operators and perhaps the most ambitious. The magnitude of its undertakings is illustrated by a fifty-million-dollar pit to be sunk in Buchanan County, Virginia, with the government of Rumania footing the bill. Continental Oil's gigantic Consolidation Coal has opened huge operations in Bell and Martin counties and plans still others. A. T. Massey Coal Company employs hundreds of men in Martin County, and South-East Coal in Letcher is steadily expanding its already huge operations, funded in part by "Consol," its largest shareholder, and by Japanese steel companies. McCulloch Oil and the W. R. Grace Corporation have acquired important holdings, and the utilities are following the lead of Duke Power in Harlan and are seeking to produce coal in their own pits for their own furnaces. In so doing the electric power companies are emulating United States Steel, Bethlehem Steel, National Steel, Republic Steel, and International Harvester which learned long ago that it was foolish to depend on unreliable small firms for their fuel requirements.

It is probable that another half-dozen years will see the map of eastern Kentucky liberally splotched with these large stable producers, each sending out several million tons annually. Some will be financed by Japanese and German industrialists and others will be sponsored by rural electric cooperatives, municipally owned power plants, and the TVA. Their employees will draw high wages, work in comparatively safe circumstances, and enjoy retirement pensions in their old age. In time they will return to the fold of the United Mine Workers, thereby adding an additional element of stability and order to those induced by relatively ample funding and long-term production contracts. The marginal operators will slowly disappear as the industry is swallowed up by the giants, taking with them some impressive displays of immense, chrome-laden cars and fingers a-sparkle with diamonds. It is to be hoped that in their departure they will take with them, also, the greed and irresponsibility that have peopled the region with myriads of paupers, cripples, and hopelessly ill people. In the disappearance of these small, independent operators the hills will trade much of their color and individuality for more dependable markets, higher wages, and less erratic social and economic norms. At the same time, the economic and political mastery of the territory may pass into the hands of entities so gigantic and so heavily financed as to assure their complete mastery for many years.

What this basic realignment of the Appalachian coal industry seems to foretell is a new era of relative economic stability which will be upset much less frequently than in the past, and then only by major shifts in national and international markets. It will bring an enlarged tax base for the support of local services and facilities. In short, it signifies that the basic and abundant resources of this huge segment of Kentucky have become indispensable to immense industries in the United States and abroad, and the Commonwealth can benefit from this situation as its voters and officials may require. In the world of the 1980s and 1990s the Kentucky mountain region can blunder along as in earlier years, sustained by welfare payments and state subsidies or it can pursue policies leading to self-supporting viability. There are attainable alternatives to failure and backwardness so that if Kentucky remains near the bottom of the list of states in any major category it will be out of choice. We will have embraced failure for its own sake.

As our second century draws to a close Kentuckians should resolve to take a careful look at their situation and needs and move with foresight and intelligence to make Kentucky the most progressive in the Union. In the early years of its history a newcomer looked at "Kaintuckee's" magnificent forests, vast canebrakes, glittering bluegrass meadows, broad alluvial bottomlands, rich soils, glittering streams, and teeming wildlife, and with a sigh of satisfaction observed that "Heaven is a Kentucky of a place!" The generations have sullied the reality, but we can recapture the magic of the old dream.

If Kentuckians are to move their state to the forefront, they must generate effective new leadership. A rebirth of public concern and constructive citizenship would retire the sellouts and special-interest lackeys and bring to the fore men and women capable of tackling the state's problems with understanding, confidence, hopefulness, and zeal. After all, the politicians mirror the people who elect them and if one is sordid and corrupt the other can lay no claim to virtue.

The state—its officials and public—should inventory the state's resources and devise an equitable tax system that will fall on all parts of the state, as evenly and uniformly as is humanly possible. Outmoded and useless governmental relics should be abandoned, including numerous antiquated offices. Counties and school districts should be strengthened, charged with greater responsibilities and consolidated into units of much larger size. The reorganization should aim at effective government at all levels, administered by competent people subject to continuing scrutiny and to prompt removal for inefficiency or nonfeasance. We have learned a lot about governmental improvement, and a decent regard for our posterity requires that it be carried into effect.

The struggle for school improvement is endless and should be turned into a determined quest for better teaching. This may require the abolition of colleges of education, with teachers educated in liberal arts colleges. We should turn our campuses into centers of advanced learning, and costly hordes of nonlearners should be channeled into manual callings where their energies can produce sorely needed goods and services. Education should lie in hard tangible subjects, sloughing off the soft and costly slush that turns out many graduates who cannot write, read, or spell. The state can easily support a scaled-down and toned-up system of this kind, and the improved quality will spread benefits into every community.

Once our schools teach us the magnitude of our resources our inventiveness can lead us to better ways of using them. Coal may be withdrawn from the earth by processes far less damaging than any we have known in the past and be used within the state in plastics, medicines, and chemicals. Our woods may be converted to furniture and prefabricated housing. Research programs in our universities may tame our worst scourges, converting themselves into important medical centers in the process. The possibilities of learning while we do and doing while we learn are measureless, and we can still tackle our future amid adequate space and marvelous natural beauty. Most of our mistakes can still be corrected, a hopeful circumstance that will decline with each passing day. If we have a hope for greatness we will think in large terms and act accordingly. The state's old chains of ignorance were fashioned out of even older chains of conservatism, an almost mindless rejection of the untried and promising. On a roadless, schoolless frontier both were tenable, but in a state laced with superhighways and sprinkled with campuses, libraries, and television stations, they can no longer be endured. In our fast-moving century a state surges to the fore or falls to the rear, and either process requires little time.

The Arab states have resolved to use their vast but dwindling fuel resources to build rich, verdant, and progressive countries. Despite the discomfort their actions cause us Americans they are, of course, wise to do it and we should commend and aid them in the task. If they succeed the whole world will benefit from their triumph. We in Kentucky should do no less. Our resources, too, are essential to the progress and well-being of the world; the world knows it and prepares to pay our price. As matters now stand the Arabs work to turn their desert lands green while we reduce much of our green land to desert. The world is willing to play the game either way, but Kentuckians alone will make the ultimate decisions. The dice of destiny are in our hands alone.

# A Suggested Bibliography

Bethell, Thomas N. *The Hurricane Creek Massacre*. New York: Harper & Row, 1972.

Bowman, Mary Jean, and Haynes, W. Warren. *Resources and People in East Kentucky: Problems and Potentials of a Lagging Economy*. Baltimore, Md.: Johns Hopkins Press, 1963.

Braun, E. Lucy. *Deciduous Forests of Eastern North America*. Facsimile of the 1950 ed. New York: Hafner Pub. Co., 1972.

Breckinridge, Mary. *Wide Neighborhoods: A Story of the Frontier Nursing Service*. New York: Harper & Row, 1952.

Brooks, Maurice. *The Appalachians*. Boston: Houghton Mifflin, 1965.

Campbell, John C. *The Southern Highlander and His Homeland*. Reprint ed. Lexington, Ky.: University Press of Kentucky, 1969.

Caruso, John A. *The Appalachian Frontier: America's First Surge Westward*. Indianapolis, Ind.: Bobbs-Merrill, 1959.

Coles, Robert. *The South Goes North*. Boston: Little, Brown, 1971.

Doddridge, Joseph. *Notes on the Settlement and Indian Wars*. Reprint of 1824 ed. Parsons, W. Va.: McClain Printing Co., 1960.

Dreiser, Theodore, et al. *Harlan Miners Speak: Report on Terrorism in the Kentucky Coal Fields*. Reprint of 1932 ed. New York: Da Capo Press, 1970.

Ely, William. *The Big Sandy Valley: A History of the People and Country from the Earliest Settlement to the Present Time*. Reprint of 1887 ed. Baltimore, Md.: Genealogical Pub. Co., 1969.

Federal Writers' Project. *Kentucky: A Guide to the Bluegrass State*. Reprint ed. New York: Somerset Pub., 1939.

Fetterman, John. *Stinking Creek*. New York: Dutton, 1967.

Fiske, John. *Old Virginia and Her Neighbors*. Boston: Houghton Mifflin, 1897.

Ford, Thomas R., ed. *The Southern Appalachian Region: A Survey*. Lexington, Ky.: University of Kentucky Press, 1962.

Gazaway, Rena. *The Longest Mile*. Garden City, N.Y.: Doubleday, 1969.

*Guide to the Medicinal Plants of Appalachia*. United States Department of Agriculture Forest Service Research Paper NE-138. Washington, D.C.: Government Printing Office, 1969.

Handlin, Oscar. *The Uprooted*. 2d ed., enl. Boston: Little, Brown, 1973.

Hirsch, Nathaniel D. Mitron. *An Experimental Study of the East Kentucky Mountaineers*. Genetic Psychology Monographs 3, no. 3 (Worcester, Mass.: Clark University, 1928).

Huddle, J. W., et al. *Coal Reserves of Eastern Kentucky*. Geological Survey Bulletin 1120. Washington, D.C.: Government Printing Office, 1963.

Kephart, Horace. *Our Southern Highlanders*. New and enl. ed. New York: Macmillan, 1922.

Looff, David H. *Appalachia's Children: The Challenge of Mental Health*. Lexington, Ky.: University Press of Kentucky, 1971.

McAllister, J. Gray, and Guerrant, Grace Owings. *Edward O. Guerrant: Apostle to the Southern Highlanders*. Richmond, Va.: Richmond Press, 1950.

*Medical Survey of the United States Coal Industry*. Washington, D.C.: Government Printing Office, 1947.

*Mineral Resources of the Appalachian Region*. United States Geological Survey Paper 580. Washington,

D.C.: Government Printing Office, 1960.

Morris, Homer Lawrence. *The Plight of the Bituminous Coal Miner*. Philadelphia: University of Pennsylvania Press, 1934.

Niles, John Jacob. *The Ballad Book*. New York: Bromhall House Press, 1960.

Noble, George Washington. *Behold He Cometh in the Clouds: An Autobiography*. Hazel Green, Ky.: Hazel Green Herald, 1912.

*North Carolina: Heads of Families at the First Census of the United States Taken in the Year 1790*. Reprint ed. Baltimore, Md.: Genealogical Pub. Co., 1973.

Peterson, Bill. *Coaltown Revisited: An Appalachian Notebook*. Chicago: Regnery, 1972.

Plunkett, H. Dudley, and Bowman, Mary Jean. *Elites and Change in the Kentucky Mountains*. Lexington, Ky.: University Press of Kentucky, 1973.

Raine, James W. *Land of Saddle-Bags: A Study of the Mountain People of Appalachia*. Reprint of 1924 ed. Detroit: Singing Tree Press, 1969.

Reed, Louis. *Warning in Appalachia: A Study of Wirt County, West Virginia*. Parsons, W. Va.: McClain Printing Co., 1967.

Roberts, Bruce and Nancy. *Where Time Stood Still: A Portrait of Appalachia*. New York: Crowell-Collier, 1970.

Stern, Philip, and De Vincent, George. *The Shame of a Nation*. New York: Astor-Honor, 1965.

Surface, Bill. *The Hollow*. New York: Coward-McCann, 1971.

Toynbee, Arnold. *A Study of History*. London: Oxford University Press, 1947.

Weller, Jack E. *Yesterday's People: Life in Contemporary Appalachia*. Lexington, Ky.: University of Kentucky Press, 1965.

Withers, Alexander Scott. *Chronicles of Border Warfare*. Reprint of 1829 ed. Parsons, W. Va.: McClain Printing Co., 1961.